Philosophy of Religion for A2 Level

Also by Michael B. Wilkinson & Hugh N. Campbell:

Philosophy of Religion for AS Level

Philosophy of Religion for A2 Level

Michael B. Wilkinson

&

Hugh N. Campbell

continuum

Published by Continuum International Publishing Group

The Tower Building	80 Maiden Lane
11 York Road	Suite 704
London	New York
SE1 7NX	NY 10038

www.continuumbooks.com

First published 2009
Reprinted 2010 (twice)

British Library Cataloguing-in-Publication Data
A catalogue record for this book is available from the British Library.

ISBN-13: PB: 978-0-8264-2271-2

Typeset by RefineCatch Limited, Bungay, Suffolk
Printed and bound in Great Britain by the MPG Books Group

Contents

Introduction

This book, like its predecessor, is a contribution to a continuing debate in wide areas in the Philosophy of Religion. It is an intrinsically exciting subject – increased numbers of students are studying it at A Level, and scholarship is developing the subject in many new and previously unconsidered directions.

No single text can deal adequately with all these developments, but we have, as far as possible, taken care to pay attention to the latest research. Too many introductory books appear to reflect the state of thought as it was twenty or thirty years ago, as if unaware that this, like all subjects, moves on. In our AS book, for example, we took account of the significance of D. Z. Phillips' *The Problem of Evil and the Problem of God*, from 2004, a detailed assault on the type of soul-making theodicy which many were beginning to take for granted. In the present work, you will find references to books published as recently as 2008 where these seem to us relevant.

We have also tried to correct errors we find continually repeated elsewhere, and which we have seen repeatedly in students' essays. Among many prevalent myths we have attempted to correct are:

- The belief that falsification is about meaning;
- The idea that eschatological verification will determine post-mortem whether our previous beliefs are true or false;
- The notion that Gilbert Ryle was a materialist;
- The curious accusation that D. Z. Philips and Gareth Moore are or were anti-realists.

On the 'anti-realists', the subject at this level has suffered from endless claims about the notion. We repeat a point made by our last book: the concept is widely mis-understood and is not required at this level. However, for readers who do want to know, we have tried to clear up the muddle in the Stretch and Challenge section of Chapter One.

As in the previous book, we have provided Stretch and Challenge material, clearly identified, at the end of various chapters. These enable you to take the debate on, but we have tried to give enough material for you to think about.

This subject is, essentially, a debate. With two authors, this creates interesting possibilities. Interests are not identical, though our working has been extraordinarily harmonious. Our philosophical interests overlap, but are not identical. Hugh, for example, is fascinated by the Science and Religion debate – Michael is not, thinking it largely the result of conceptual muddle. Michael loves the technical side of the subject, while Hugh is more interested in the theological implications of ideas. The strategy we chose will be evident as you read. Hugh has dealt with Boethius and the Divine Attributes, as well as the lengthy chapter on the Afterlife which concludes this book. Additionally, Hugh wrote all the advice and exercises at the end of each chapter. Each of us has commented on and made additions to the other's work. We thought it appropriate to retain the two tones of voice – it gives the book, we hope, the feeling of a conversation, for that is what the writing has been. And it is a conversation in which we want you to join.

We insist at various places that you must be prepared to reach your own judgements – to think about the issues. The subject is not about simply learning lists of arguments – the excellent student *reflects* on them and *engages* with them. We have not been afraid in places to do the same. This subject is not reducible to bullet-points. Nevertheless, we have provided, as with our AS book, extensive revision notes as an appendix. These are an additional aid to memory, but are not, and are not intended to be, a substitute for your own careful reflection.

* * *

As ever, our thanks are owed to various friends and colleagues. Vicky Bunting, OCR Principal Examiner for Buddhism and Hinduism, checked our material on reincarnation. Dr Stephen Robinson of Sussex Downs College has acted as sounding board for many of the philosophical arguments in the text. Edna Wilkinson has acted as our eagle-eyed guardian of grammar and second reader of the proofs. Discussion with various philosophers, past and present, has contributed to ideas herein. Often it has been a chance remark which has led us to particular arguments. Mark Wynn, John Cottingham, Anthony O'Hear, Peter Vardy, John Frye, Father Jonathan How, Michael Durrant, Vincent Brümmer and Patrick Sherry have each, unawares, contributed to the book through their conversation. A particular debt is owed to the late D. Z. Phillips, that larger than life figure, who stimulated so much discussion. His opposition to anti-realism was volubly developed over several glasses of wine (and the odd beer) in a bar in Leuven in 2004. Also, special thanks are owed, posthumously, to Father John Fitzgerald, Czesław Lejewski and D. P. Henry.

The stimulus for the book came from the admirable and endlessly supportive Haaris Naqvi, our editor at Continuum Books. He and the copy editors keep us both fairly honest and on schedule. The guidance we have received from them means that both books have fewer errors than might otherwise be the case, which means we have no excuse for remaining errors, save our own carelessness.

As ever, our thanks go to the long–suffering members of our families for putting up with us during the writing. Tina, Rhiannon and Angharad have encouraged

Hugh throughout, while Michael has been chivvied and encouraged by Imelda. An interesting contribution was made by Tweazel, the Wilkinson cat. Occasional wanderings across the keyboard, and once choosing to sit on it, created new and interesting logical symbols and formulae, which, alas, we have chosen to omit.

As ever, this book is for our students – past, present and future.

Michael B. Wilkinson
Hugh N. Campbell

Preparing for the Examination

After each chapter you will find an exercise in the format prescribed for the examination. At A2, this consists of an essay question, and we strongly recommend that you study carefully our advice on how to write a philosophy essay. This gives advice not just for your work at this stage, but for your future studies at University. As examiners, we see many answers which not merely fail to answer questions but which are badly organized – perhaps random lists of points. What examiners want to see is that you have answered the question set, not merely by listing the views of others but *engaging* with these ideas, demonstrating that you have thought about them for yourself.

Examiners begin marking with one clear idea in their minds: 'Has this candidate answered the question set?' If you do not, however good the material be used, you will not achieve much. Many people wrongly think that examinations test how much you know. They do not. They test *whether you can answer the question.* Of course, in answering the question you need accurate information to support the answer, but accurate information by itself does not guarantee good marks. You must have *selected* the correct material, organized it well and really engaged with it. In your revision, you must not just *learn* arguments as if they were facts, like the names of the bones in the body: what you need to do is to think about them, to argue with them, to test them, if necessary to destruction. Remember that Philosophy is an argument, a debate, a conversation. Candidates who achieve the highest marks join the debate: they do not just watch from the sidelines.

Marking the Examination

Examiners award two marks for each essay: the first (AO1) out of 25, the second (AO2) out of 10.

Firstly, they ask themselves how good an answer is to the question set. This is always the first consideration, because it determines the highest mark you can achieve. It does not matter how excellent the material you have given, if it does not answer the question, it will not be rewarded. It never ceases to amaze – or to sadden – examiners how many candidates each year perform poorly because they have learned masses of stuff, but just didn't answer the question. Too often, candidates – sometimes whole centres – pre-prepare answers which will be trotted out regardless. A good example is when examiners ask a specific question about miracles. Suppose the question is 'Assess Maurice Wiles' reasons for rejecting miracles.' The examiner's heart sinks when she sees another all-purpose essay on miracles ('here's one I prepared earlier'), trotting dutifully through Aquinas, Hume, Uncle Tom Cobbleigh, with perhaps a paragraph on Wiles. Everything in it may be true and accurate, but the candidate does not give any evidence of having directly addressed the question.

Let us look at the grid used for assessing AO1:

Mark Band	Mark	Description
0	0	Absent/no relevant material
1	1–5	Almost completely ignores the question • Little relevant material • Some concepts inaccurate • Shows little knowledge of technical terms Communication: often unclear or disorganized
2	6–10	Focuses on the general topic rather than directly on the question • Knowledge limited and partly accurate • Limited understanding • Selection often inappropriate • Limited use of technical terms Community: some clarity and organization

Mark Band	Mark	Description
3	11–15	Satisfactory attempt to address the question • Some accurate knowledge • Appropriate understanding • Some successful selection of material • Some accurate use of technical terms Communication: some clarity and organization
4	16–20	A good attempt to address the question • Accurate knowledge • Good understanding • Good selection of material • Technical terms mostly accurate Communication: generally clear and organized
5	21–25	An excellent attempt to address the question showing understanding and engagement with the material • Very high level of ability to select and deploy relevant information • Accurate use of technical terms Communication: answer is well constructed and organized

Notice how important it is to answer the question. The heading to each box sets the maximum band you can achieve. If you wrote everything you knew about miracles, as so many do, how would you mark it?

Remember the examiner's question: has this candidate answered the question? Remember that only one paragraph was on Wiles. What would you be thinking, if you were marking it? The answer is simple – Level 2 at best, and not very far into that. Some might argue the candidate had almost completely ignored the question, but examiners would credit anything relevant they could find in the little bit directly relevant to the question. Pages of the answer – and some candidates needlessly write colossal amounts – would attract no reward at all, as they would not be on the question. It is worth being aware that the examination is not an exercise in showing how much you can write in the time allotted – it is simply about answering the question. Two well-directed pages can be (and usually are) much better than 15 sides of everything you ever heard about miracles. Examiners set questions geared to perhaps 40 minutes of writing at normal speed. If you have written 15 pages, somewhere you will almost certainly have failed to make the material relevant. When preparing students for examinations, I often say, 'If someone found a page of an essay by you in the street, would she be able to work out from that page of your answer what the question was?, If the answer is "no", there is something wrong with it.' It's a good notion to keep in mind in the examination room. Do not be put off by someone else continually asking for another few sheets of extra paper: stick to the question.

Look again at this grid, paying particular attention to the heading in each box. Consider a candidate who has learned every argument accurately and who listed all those arguments, all relevantly. Which level would you give? There would be a case, if the selection were substantial and relevant, for awarding a mark somewhere in level 4, but none for level 5. This would be a candidate who had *learned* the material, perhaps as a list of facts, but not one who *engaged* and revealed *understanding*. The latter comes from reflection, from really developing your own judgements. Candidates who achieve Level 5 often include fewer facts than some at Level 4, but everything they write is argued for, considered, weighed and is directly relevant to the question.

We suggest that you use the grid to reflect critically on every piece of writing you do. This will give you essential and invaluable practice. Notice also the importance of using technical terms with precision. Too many candidates handicap themselves by failure to use basic philosophical terms (such as 'proof', 'refute', 'logical', 'meaningful', 'inductive' and so on) without any thought about their correct meaning. (Give some thought to legible handwriting also: if the examiner cannot read it, she will assume it's wrong. If it is just about legible, the flow of reading is interrupted and the force of your overall argument suffers, which could affect your mark.)

AO2

For this mark, examiners assess how well you have managed to reach a judgement, to explain, evaluate or to discuss. If you are asked to discuss, consider or evaluate something, you are being asked whether you believe it is true, and why. Simply to say 'I believe . . .' is not philosophical – philosophers insist always on giving reasons.

A list of points does not constitute an argument. Simply to say: 'x says . . ., however y disagrees by saying . . .' does not mean that you have *engaged* with the argument: you have simply noted the *fact* that Buggins says this and Baggins disagreed with him. What do you say about their disagreement? What is your judgement about their dispute? Why have you reached that judgement?

It is important to note here, yet again, that if you have not *thought* about the issues as you have worked your way through the course, you cannot hope in the few minutes of the examination to develop your ideas from scratch. As you work, and as you revise, never just *learn* arguments. *Think* about them. Consider which convince you, and which do not, and ask yourself *why* you are convinced. The best candidates have always thought through the issues. Weaker ones have learned them, but not made them part of their intellectual life. Work on reaching a conclusion, with reasons, showing awareness of alternative views and why you reject them.

The mark scheme for this part is:

Mark Band	Mark	Description
0	0	Absent/no argument
1	1–2	Very little argument or justification of viewpoint • Little or no successful analysis Communication: often unclear or disorganized
2	3–4	An attempt to sustain an argument and justify a viewpoint • Some analysis, but not successful • Views asserted but not successfully justified Communication: some clarity and organization
3	5–6	The argument is sustained and justified • Some successful analysis which may be implicit Communication: some clarity and organization
4	7–8	A good attempt at using evidence to sustain an argument • Some successful and clear analysis • Might put more than one point of view Communication: generally clear and organized
5	9–10	An excellent attempt which uses a range of evidence to sustain an argument • Comprehends the demands of the question • Shows understanding and critical analysis of different viewpoints Communication: answer is well constructed and organized

Notice again that the levels are directed to how well you create an argument *which answers the question*. Notice also how those most highly rewarded are not those who just *put* different points of view they have learned (Level 4, or just asserted an opinion – Level 2). The best have demonstrated their own understanding and thoughtfulness.

Doing well in the examination is always a matter of doing the simple things well. Ask always, what precisely am I asked to do? What is the precise instruction? Obey that, using appropriate knowledge, and you cannot fail.

Timeline

Pythagoras (fl.530)

Heraclitus (c. sixth century BC)

Parmenides (c.520–c.450)

Socrates (469–399 BC)

Plato (427–347 BC)

Aristotle (384–322 BC)

Cicero (106–43 BC)

Jesus Christ (c.4 BC–c.29 AD)

St Paul (??–AD 64/67)

St Irenaeus (c.130–c.202)

Origen (c.185–254)

Plotinus (205–c.269)

Porphyry (c.232–c.305)

St Augustine of Hippo (354–430)

Boethius (c.480–524)

Al-Kindi (c.801–866)

John Scotus Eriugena (c.810–c.877)

Al-Farabi (870–950)

Avicenna (Ibn Sina) (980–1037)

St Anselm of Canterbury (1033–1109)

Al-Ghazali (1058/9–1111)

Abelard (1079–1142)

Averröes (1126–1198)

Moses Maimonides (1124–1198)

St Albertus Magnus (St Albert the Great) (c.1200–1280)

St Bonaventure (1221–1274)

St Thomas Aquinas (1224/5–1274)

William of Ockham (c.1285–c.1349)

Erasmus of Rotterdam (1465–1536)

Martin Luther (1483–1536)

John Calvin (1509–1564)

Archbishop James Ussher (1581–1656)

Hugo Grotius (1583–1645)

Thomas Hobbes (1588–1679)

Rene Descartes (1596–1650)

Baruch Spinoza (1632–1677)

John Locke (1632–1704)

Sir Isaac Newton (1642–1727)

Gottfried Leibniz (1646–1716)

George Berkeley (1685–1753)

David Hume (1711–1776)

Immanuel Kant (1724–1804)

William Paley (1743–1805)

Jeremy Bentham (1748–1832)

Georg Hegel (1770–1831)

John Henry, Cardinal Newman (1801–1890)

John Stuart Mill (1806–1873)

Charles Darwin (1809–1882)

Philip Gosse (1810–1888)

Søren Kierkegaard (1813–1855)

Karl Marx (1818–1883)

Frederick Temple, Archbishop of Canterbury (1821–1902)

Franz Brentano (1838–1917)

William James (1842–1910)

Friedrich Nietzsche (1844–1900)

Gottlob Frege (1848–1925)

Sir James Frazer (1854–1941)

Sigmund Freud (1856–1939)

Alfred North Whitehead (1861–1947)

Bertrand Russell (1872–1970)

Jan Łukasiewicz (1878–1956)

Martin Buber (1878–1965)

William Temple, Archbishop of Canterbury (1881–1944)

Pierre Teilhard de Chardin (1881–1955)

Moritz Schlick (1882–1936)

Rudolf Bultmann (1884–1976)

Tadeusz Kotarbiński (1886–1981)

Paul Tillich (1886–1965)

Martin Heidegger (1889–1976)

Ludwig von Wittgenstein (1889–1951)

Rudolf Carnap (1891–1970)

Charles Hartshorne (1897–2000)

Gilbert Ryle (1900–1976)

R. B. Braithwaite (1900–90)

Karl Popper (1902–1994)

Karl Rahner (1904–1984)

Dorothy Emmett (1904–2000)

Rush Rhees (1905–1989)

Jean-Paul Sartre (1905–1980)

F. C. Copleston (1907–1994)

A. J. Ayer (1910–1989)

J. L. Austin (1911–1960)

Norman Malcolm (1911–1990)

Czesław Lejewski (1913–2001)

Peter Geach (1916–)

J. L. Mackie (1917–1981)

Basil Mitchell (1917–)

G. E. M. (Elizabeth) Anscombe (1919–2001)

R. M. Hare (1919–2002)

John Hick (1922–)

Anthony Flew (1923–)

Maurice Wiles (1923–2005)

Sir Michael Dummett (1925–)

Peter Winch (1926–1997)

Herbert McCabe (1926–2001)

Anthony Kenny (1931–)

Alvin Plantinga (1932–)

Vincent Brümmer (1932–)

Dewi Zephaniah Phillips (1934–2006)

Richard Swinburne (1934–)

Don Cupitt (1934–)

Robert Nozick (1938–2002)

Keith Ward (1938–)

Peter Atkins (1940–)

Michael Ruse (1940–)

Richard Dawkins (1941–)

Peter van Inwagen (1942–)

John Cottingham (1943–)

Peter Vardy (1945–)

Eberhard Herrman (1946–)

Michael Behe (1952–)

Alister McGrath (1953–)

Problems of Knowledge and Knowing God 1

Introduction

According to the Bible, in verses famously set by Handel, in *Messiah*:

> I know that my Redeemer liveth, and that He shall stand at the latter day upon the earth: and though worms destroy this body, yet in my flesh shall I see God. *Job* xix, 25–6.

In a sense, it is the implications of those beliefs that form the core of this book. But what does it mean to make to such a statement. Consider ordinary sentences:

- I know that $2 + 2 = 4$.
- I know that the Matterhorn is near Zermatt.
- I know you.
- I know that I have faith in you.

In those four sentences, the verb 'know' has a very different meaning. In the first, to know that $2 + 2 = 4$ is an *a priori* truth. I know that it is true because I know the meanings of the terms and understand the assumptions of the decimal system of arithmetic on which that truth rests.

The second is more problematic. I do know that the Matterhorn is near Zermatt, but how might that sentence be understood? I might know it because I have stood on its slopes, as I have: the term 'Matterhorn' conjures up a vivid recollection. But, for others, it is a matter of report – something known through pictures, reading or hearsay. My knowledge of the mountain involves a direct acquaintance: but someone else might know the truth of the sentence in ways I cannot. I might, for example, have failed to note the name of the village at the foot of the mountain, yet know unmistakably from the distinctive shape that this mountain is the Matterhorn. A geography student might know that the Zermatt lies beside the Matterhorn, know far more about the geological makeup, height, population etc. than have I, yet have no idea of the appearance of either. The sense in which he can be said to know the truth of the sentence is different in important ways from my knowing it. Much that I might claim to know about God is not dissimilar from that geographer's understanding. I have no direct knowledge of what God looks like – indeed, I have no knowledge of what Jesus looked or sounded like. The evangelists drew no pictures and wrote about Jesus without ever describing his physical appearance. If he were a typical Galilean, he would have been short by modern standards, clean-shaven, talking Aramaic, and, as a Nazarene, a little colloquial Greek, each with a strong accent. But, if he were a typical Galilean, I would not know him among others. To say that I know Jesus, seems, at first sight, similar to the knowledge of the geography student who knows the facts about the Matterhorn, but who would not recognize it.

The third sentence represents another complex usage. To say that 'I know you' is ambiguous in many ways. It might mean simply that I recognize you, having once met you. It might, on the other hand, mean that I know a great deal about you. In a certain tone, it might mean something else. When, for example, I promise my wife to buy no more books this year, her 'I know you' implies a (well-founded) scepticism about my inability to resist the lure of booksellers.

In the fourth case, to say I know that I have faith in you is to say something very special: it implies not merely an intellectual act but a kind of self-commitment – an attitude of trust. Notice too that I sometimes have faith *in* a person on very little factual knowledge: there is just something about that person which I find especially trustworthy. Asked to articulate what it is that leads to that conclusion, I might say, rather lamely, 'he has an honest face'. Of course, I know I might be mistaken – Josef Stalin was affectionately known as 'Uncle Joe' while murdering untold numbers of his fellow-citizens – but there is a claim to 'knowing' in the case of trust which is different from knowing the truth of the conclusion of a syllogism.

Claims to religious knowledge seem to involve elements of all these ways of knowing. Nevertheless, if I claim to 'know that my redeemer liveth', I at once open myself to the challenge of what it means to make that claim. Generally, to make the claim that I *know x*, I need to be able to say something about *x*, either in terms of my immediate acquaintance (as when I say 'I know Hugh Campbell') or the particular pieces of knowledge I have (facts about the Matterhorn, for instance). But that is what is not immediately to hand about God. God is in important ways unknown to us – as Herbert McCabe says:

> What I refer to as God is not any character in the drama of the universe but the author of the universe, the mystery of wisdom which we know of but cannot begin to understand, the wisdom that is the reason why there is a harmony called the universe which we can just stumblingly begin to understand. Our lives are a subplot in the story of the universe, but that story is not one we can comprehend, and it is one that often puzzles us and troubles us and sometimes outrages us. Herbert McCabe: 'Why God?', *Faith Within Reason*, Continuum 2007.

Now, if that which we claim to know is so utterly mysterious to us, can we properly be said in any sense to *know* it? To say I know God, sounds rather like saying, 'I know all about this thing I do not even begin to understand.' To *know* is surely involves understanding. I cannot be said to know about nuclear physics when I do not understand it. And, in relation to God, I can say that part of my lack of understanding is a failure to be certain about the *meaning* of the term 'God'. I know what a table is, and so understand the meaning of the word 'table'. I can use the term significantly in sentences where the word occurs. But if I cannot understand the term 'God', is there any way in which I can construct significant sentences involving the term? Does the claim about knowing that my redeemer liveth have any more content than a claim that I know the condoogle of the booglefuss?

It should be said at once that the unknowability of God is accepted by the great religions as a central truth. The continual fear is that of idolatry, which is not a matter of primitive people worshipping this stone or that temple statue, but the ever-present danger of making God in our own image. There are many who claim too easily to know the mind of God, when all they are doing is to express their own desires. It is the awareness of this danger that leads Islam to forbid the representation of God, and, among Jews, a reluctance even to use his full name. It is interesting that the Roman Catholic claim that the Pope can speak infallibly on matters involving faith and morals involves a power invoked only once[1] since the proclamation of the doctrine at the First Vatican Council of 1870. Yet, there are those who claim just to *know* what God wants.

As we shall see, it is with questions of meaning and justification with which we shall be most concerned. Some argue that religious sentences are simply meaningless, while others have different views of both meaning and justification. It is sometimes crudely said that in Philosophy there have been three great ages. From the Greeks until the end of the Middle Ages, the principal concern was metaphysical, as philosophers asked what existed (e.g. the Forms, God and so on). Then, following Descartes, philosophers turned to questions of what we can know, those of epistemology. The rise of new studies in logic and language in the twentieth century led to a concern not with what is, or what we can know, but rather with the meaning of the language we use. It was not that the older problems had been resolved but that attention turned elsewhere. As a generalization, this characterization into three ages has some value, but we should not assume that it answers all cases. For instance, philosophers such as St Anselm, Peter Abelard and Aquinas devoted much of their thought to the meaning of language, and Plato's theory of the Forms is itself an attempt to discern the meaning of abstract terms such as 'truth', 'beauty' and 'goodness'.

Justification

It is a very human instinct to want justification. If I believe I may be promoted, it is natural to seek justification for that belief, to seek out evidence that my hope is not vain. I do not want to find a dismissal notice where I had expected to hear of a new role and more money. It is natural, some might say, to want assurance that the commitment to faith was appropriate to the facts. After all, to have faith in God is life-changing and time-consuming in a way that my belief about the proximity of the Matterhorn to Zermatt is probably not, at least for me.

There is an important difference between knowing something that is true and knowing *that* it is true. For instance, someone may have awareness that everyone believes that Everest is the highest mountain – which is factually correct – without any clear memory of learning it, or of knowing how to demonstrate the truth of his belief: in short, he cannot demonstrate that his is a *justified* position. It is only true to say '*S knows* that *p*' if we have conditions of justification. By *S* we mean the subject – the person who has the knowledge – and by *p* that fact or proposition which is known.

We want to determine – if possible – what might justify saying that someone can be described as *knowing* something. To put it more formally, we are looking to fill in the blanks in the sentence:

S knows that *p* if and only if . . .

An obvious test here might be to ask whether I can answer the question of how I know the information is correct, or how I might justify my claim to know. Certainly, one would only accept someone as having knowledge when satisfactory answers can be given to these questions. We accept claims to *knowledge* only when a good answer is given – 'my mother said so', 'it was in the *Sunday Sport*', are not, for some of us, at least some of the time, sufficient answer.

Conditions of Knowledge

1. Now, it is clear that one philosophical condition of possessing knowledge is that what is claimed as knowledge is *true*. If I say that I know that the moon is made of green cheese, then those who have evidence to the contrary do not simply assert that the moon is not made of green cheese, but also that I have no claim to use the word 'knowledge'. *Ex hypothesi*, there can be no such thing as false knowledge, and people would say simply that I had belief about the moon, or that I held a green-cheese hypothesis. To formalize these points, we can say both:

   (a) if S knows that p, then it is true that p
   and
   (b) if S knows that p, then p

   So it is possible to give our first firm condition of knowledge that:

   It is true S *knows* that p if and only if p.

   Most believers would accept this, saying that they cannot *know* that god exists if He does not. Atheists would deny that religious believers have *knowledge*, as there is nothing for them to know.

2. The second condition of knowledge is *acceptance*. If I do not accept something as true, then I do not know it. It may happen to be true that I have such-and-such a waistline size, but if I refuse to accept the evidence of the tape measure, then I cannot be said to *know* it. We may summarize this easily:

   If S knows that p, then S accepts that p.

   We need to notice here that some philosophers claim that we may know something to be true while – in another sense – refusing to accept it, as, for instance, if I were secretly to buy clothes by the tape-measure rather than by my belief in the actual sylph-like nature of my figure. It is perhaps easiest to resolve these arguments by saying that acceptance involves some sort of belief that *p* is true, while recognising that some kinds of belief are not sufficient for us to assert that something can be accepted. *Belief* is a vaguer notion than *acceptance*.

   Some critics of religious belief argue that the position of believers is rather like that of the person who denies the evidence of the tape measure. As we shall see in the chapter on falsification, Flew challenges believers to say what they would accept as evidence against their beliefs.

3. The third condition is *justification*. It is sometimes said that for there to be knowledge there has to be at least 'justified true belief'. But perhaps we can be more precise than this. It might be possible to accept that someone does not have to be completely certain that *p* in order to be said to know that *p*, but it does seem necessary that he be completely *justified* in his acceptance that *p* in order to be said properly to know that *p*.

    There needs to be awareness that slight justification or some sort of justification is not enough. What I believe may happen to be true, but that is not enough for me to justify the assertion that I have knowledge. The fact that someone is guilty is not sufficient evidence to send him to prison: a court must have justification of the assertion of guilt. Philosophically the test has to be on the basis of adequate evidence, and not merely of suggestive evidence. We can express the justification condition as:

    > If *S* knows that *p*, then *S* is completely justified in accepting that *p*.

4. The fourth condition is that no false statement is involved in a case of knowledge – there must be no false premise. It would not be knowledge if we were to deduce –rightly on the logic – from 'Socrates is a man', 'All men are psychopaths', 'All psychopaths are mortal', the (factually correct) 'Socrates is mortal'. The conclusion is correct, but this cannot be held to be *knowledge* in this case, since it rests on a false premise. We may assert:

    > If *S* knows that *p*, then *S* is completely justified in accepting that *p* in some way that does not depend on any false statement.

    We now have a preliminary description of an analysis of knowledge; this may be expressed:

    > *S* knows that *p* if and only if (i) it is true that *p*, (ii) *S* accepts that *p*, (iii) *S* is completely justified in accepting that *p*, and (iv) *S* is completely justified in accepting *p* in some way that does not depend on any false statement.

These preliminary remarks give us an understanding of what it is for something to be known, but they need to be supplemented by a theory of what counts as adequate reason or justification. Today there are three major theories in common use: *Foundation* theory, *Coherence* theory and *Externalist* theory.

Theories of Justification

1. *Foundation Theory.* This holds, as the name implies, that knowledge and justification rest on some sort of foundation of the first premises of justification, these premises being basic beliefs justified in themselves, or self-justified beliefs. On these the justification for all other beliefs rests.

   This theory is advanced to avoid the problem of *infinite regress*, in which every justification would need, in its turn, to be justified.

   To foundation theorists, basic beliefs provide the evidence in terms of which all other beliefs are justified. There is no agreement about what those basic beliefs might be. Descartes argued from a foundation of *Cogito ergo sum*, but this is open to doubt on the grounds that it is not a tautology ('existing' is not a defining predicate of the concept of 'thinking', and we cannot go from 'there is a thought now' to the connected being we mean by the term 'I'). Empiricists might argue from basic beliefs about perception ('I can see something blue'), while others, such as Kant or A. J. Ayer, might prefer the more *phenomenalist* approach ('There is the appearance of something blue').

   Foundationalists tend to argue that without some such foundations, the only other possibility would be a free-floating scepticism.

   Foundationalism is advocated by some modern philosophers of religion, including Alvin Plantinga. These philosophers argue that God is the foundational belief – we cannot ask 'Why God?' We cannot go behind God. He is the foundation on which all other truths rest. On this view, it would be pointless to try to *prove* God exists – that would mean going behind the foundation. If God is the foundation or beginning we cannot, as it were, go behind him, as there would be nowhere to go. This position has been widely challenged by those who argue that God is not a self-evident truth, or, at least, as Aquinas points out, that his self-evidence cannot be self-evident to us. A trenchant modern critic of Foundationalism was D. Z. Phillips.[2] An obvious criticism is that foundationalism presupposes that a sure and certain foundation can be found. Simply because we *want* such a thing does not entail that it exists, and the fact that different types of foundationalist disagree about whether a given proposition is foundational suggests a degree of wishful thinking. Certainly, that there is a foundation to our knowledge is not an indubitable truth.

2. *Coherence Theory.* This denies any need for basic beliefs. Supporters of this view argue that justification is different from either argumentation or reasoning. There need be no basic beliefs, because all beliefs may be justified by the mutual support of a whole system of beliefs. The whole edifice of, for example, science coheres. My belief that I see something blue can be justified because there exists a coherent system of beliefs about the conditions under which it is possible to

assert the perception of blueness with which this particular instance is consistent.

To those who take a coherence view, there is no need to seek foundations: indeed, it would be pointless if indeed there are no foundations to be found. After all, I assert I am currently awake and not dreaming because my present perceptions have a mutual consistency and internal explicability absent from the experiences I call delusion or dreaming. No further justification is either sought or necessary.

Many religious believers argue that their beliefs make sense of their understanding of the world. God explains the otherwise inexplicable. The problem is that our entire understanding of the world may be mistaken. For example, our entire science may cohere with the notion that everything has a cause, but, as David Hume pointed out, just because we see the world in terms of cause and effect, it does not follow that cause and effect are actually to be found in the world – we just see it that way.

3. *Externalist Theory.* This argues that we do not need basic beliefs or internal coherence to justify knowledge. Instead, we need to make the right connection between external reality and my beliefs. When the right sort of connection is made, then I am justified in saying I have knowledge.

Such a theorist might argue that causality could create such a connection – my belief that I see something blue is caused by my seeing some external blue thing. To this approach, belief is less important than the link between the mind and the outside world.

An example of a believer in this type of theory would be the American philosopher, Robert Nozick (1938–2002), who developed a theory which he described as *tracking*. He argued that we have knowledge when the sentences we use correctly *track* reality, rather as a recording of a piece of music follows the original.

The key problem of all forms of externalism is that they require a connection of our mind with reality. But, we can never get outside our minds to check the correctness of our perceptions. It would be wonderful to step outside ourselves to judge that my impression of something corresponds with the way it really is, as we might compare a map with a landscape, but we are never in that privileged position. If I ask you whether that chair is really there, I hear you only through my senses – and those senses may have invented you as they have invented the chair. My knowledge is always mine, and that of no-one else. Externalism seems to assume the reality we cannot prove. The believer cannot get outside her mind to check that the God in whom she believes is either truly there or is as she believes.

Cognitive and Non-Cognitive Sentences

In what we have said so far, there has been an assumption that the sentences we use either have, or purport to have, some connection with reality. But not all sentences have this character. Suppose, while rushing into the bathroom (late for college again!), you happen to stub your bare toe on the corner of the bath. You may exclaim, 'Oh, dearie, dearie me!', or 'Oh, my ears and whiskers!' or some such thing. Now, if you are overheard by a parent, the one thing that would not be said to you would be: 'That's not true'. Rather, a parent will say, 'We don't use that language in this house', or, 'Wash your mouth out with soap and water', or even, solicitously, 'Are you all right?' To your sudden words, questions of truth and falsity are irrelevant. In the same way, if I say, 'Go and wash your mouth out with soap and water', you may say, 'No, I won't!' but never, 'That's a lie'.

Philosophers recognize two types of sentences: *cognitive* and *non-cognitive.*

A *cognitive* sentence is one about which it is appropriate to ask whether it is true or false: a *non-cognitive* sentence is one about which it is not appropriate to ask that question. Notice that a cognitive sentence is not necessarily a true one. For example, the sentence, 'London is the capital of Germany' is cognitive and untrue. It is appropriate to ask *whether it is true,* and that is why it is cognitive.

Orders, commands, curses, prayers, are all – probably – non-cognitive.

But, sometimes, it is not obvious from the structure of a sentence whether it is cognitive or not. Take the sentence: 'My great grandfather was a pirate.' It looks cognitive, and it would be if I were purporting to tell you my family history. But, suppose that sentence were the opening of my great new novel. In those circumstances, it would be inappropriate to ask whether it happened to be true. We do not accuse students of literature of being natural liars or enthusiasts for lies. To ask whether *Pride and Prejudice* or *Harry Potter and the Philosopher's Stone* are true or false is to ask the wrong kind of question in the circumstances.

An important question is whether religious sentences are cognitive or not. Many thinkers, such as Richard Dawkins, obviously take the bulk of religious sentences as cognitive but obviously false. For Dawkins, the believer speaks that which is untrue. But, notice, most believers would argue that to say 'God exists' is to utter a true statement, asserted as true. Believers generally believe that when they talk of God's action in the world, they are referring to a state of affairs they hold to be true and which atheists hold to be false.

But, in recent years, there have been arguments that suggest that religious sentences are non-cognitive. In the course of the book we shall investigate some of these claims.

STRETCH AND CHALLENGE

Few topics cause as much misunderstanding as the modern notion of anti-realism. Much nonsense has been written about it, and it is a position widely misunderstood. Some authors even go so far as to equate anti-realism with non-cognitivism, which is absurd.[3] As a piece of examination advice, if you are at all uncertain about the notion, leave it out of your answers. Examiners do not expect you to understand concepts which so many textbooks in the subject misunderstand so thoroughly.

The term 'anti-realism' was coined by Professor Sir Michael Dummett, (1925–) who succeeded Sir Alfred Ayer (A. J. Ayer) as Wykeham Professor of Logic at Oxford University. (It should be said that Dummett is difficult to read, but you might find his Gifford Lectures *Thought and Reality*[4] valuable, not least because it contains some of his thoughts on truth and God – Dummett is a devout Catholic). Dummett opposes justificationism, that is, the attempt to find an external or foundational justification for claiming knowledge, the obvious problem being that we cannot step outside our minds to check our basic understanding. Instead, what we seek are assertability conditions. That sounds complex, but think of a child learning language. He is never in a position to make the connections with the world to check that things really are there, or that there is justification for a foundational belief, or even that he *has* a foundational belief: what he learns instead are the rules under which he may use the sentence. There are rules which permit him to say: 'There is a duck' in some circumstances but not in others. To use the sentence correctly is to learn the conventions of a very complex language structure.

A very helpful way to think of this is to consider the language of jokes, such as 'Knock, knock,' jokes. A good example would be:

Q. What is grey, and has a trunk?
A. A mouse going on holiday.

Now, if we consider the joke, everything hangs on the meaning of the words. We know what we mean by the word 'mouse', 'grey' and so on. It is wholly understandable, *but* bears no relation, or almost no relation, to reality. It is independent of the reality of the world, and is not justified by some relation to the world.

Dummett devotes much attention to what he considers over-simple assumptions about sentences as bi-valent, that is, either true or false. Sentences about the past, for example, are not obviously provable as true or false, mathematical sentences such as $7 + 5 = 12$ are not justified as true by some relationship to objects, but by systems of rules – assertability conditions which enable us to use the sentence properly. I may use the sentence '$7 + 5 = 12$' properly in decimal arithmetic, but not in binary.

In his paper 'Realism'[5] Dummett argues that realism and anti-realism should be seen as opposed theories of *meaning*, rather than of knowledge of the world. He argues that a realist is someone who wants us to understand the meanings of sentences in terms of their truth-conditions (the situations that must be true for the sentence to be true) while an anti-realist holds that meanings are to be understood by reference to assertability-conditions (the circumstances in which we would be justified in asserting them). The argument would then become one of how we are to understand meaning and not about our relationship to the world, whether that world is real or imagined.

A common error about anti-realism is to assume that a given theory is either realist or anti-realist. Peter Vardy, for example, treats realism and anti-realism as opposed positions, even inaccurately associating the latter, incorrectly, with coherence theory – which is justificationist![6] Dummett rejects such an understanding:

. . . realism is a definite doctrine. Its denial, by contrast, may take any one of numerous possible forms, each of which is a variety of anti-realism concerning the given subject matter: the colourless term anti-realism is apt as a signal that it denotes not a specific doctrine but a rejection of doctrine.[7]

In recent years, some philosophers have considered both realism (in the justificationist sense) and anti-realism inadequate understandings, and have attempted to move to wider perspectives.

The major source of confusion, for many, is a confusion of terms. The Anglican theologian, Don Cupitt, adopted a point of view often called *non-realism* (or 'theological non-realism') which is not concerned with asserting the objective existence of God, (which Cupitt calls 'theological realism') but with the meaning of God in people's lives. For Cupitt and his followers (many in the Sea of Faith movement) God exists in us – faith is a stance on life. Cupitt opposes theological realism to 'expressivism'.[8] For him, God has no objective reality:

> The Christian doctrine of God just is Christian spirituality in coded form, for God is a symbol that represents to us everything that spirituality requires of us and promises to us.[9]

What matters for Cupitt is what the God-concept expresses. To live within a sense of the meaning of God transforms this life.

It sometimes appears that writers such as Vardy confuse the realism versus anti-realism debate, which is around justificationism, with the theological realism versus *non-realism* debate. Vardy for example, considers D. Z. Phillips an anti-realist, a position vehemently denied by the latter. Phillips thought emphatically that God was real and Perfect Love. On the realism/non realism debate, he commented:

> Theological non-realism is as empty as theological realism. Both terms are battle-cries in a confused philosophical and theological debate.[10]

For Phillips, the search for God was a *religious* rather than a *philosophical* quest – the task of the philosopher being to clarify terms – but nonetheless real for all that.[11] But remember, if in doubt, leave it out.

Notes

1. In 1950, Pope Pius XII promulgated the doctrine of the Assumption of Mary into heaven, a belief long held in the Roman Catholic Church. Papal Infallibility extends to matters of faith and morals only, when the Pope speaks *ex cathedra*, that is from the chair of Peter. No Pope has spoken *ex cathedra* on moral matters, or on which horse will win the 2.30 at Kempton Park.
2. D. Z. Phillips (1988) *Faith After Foundationalism* (Routledge).
3. See for example: Sarah Tyler and Gordon Reid: *Religious Studies*, Philip Allen Updates, 2002, p. 115. The muddle about coherence theory is present throughout their work.
4. Oxford University Press, 2006.
5. Michael Dummett (1978) *Truth and Other Enigmas*, Duckworth.
6. See *The Puzzle of God*, HarperCollins 1990, or *What is Truth*, John Hunt, 2003, especially pp. 12–29.
7. Michael Dummett (1994) *The Logical Basis of Metaphysics*, Duckworth, p. 4.

8. Cupitt's position is explained perhaps most clearly in his *Taking Leave of God*, SCM, 2001.
9. *Ibid.*, p. 15.
10. D. Z. Phillips (1993) *Wittgenstein and Religion* (Macmillan), p. 35.
11. See obituary by Patrick Sherry: also personal conversation with the author, September 2004. Vardy, and others, also suggest that Father Gareth Moore is anti-realist. (They seem to mean non-realist.) This seems improbable:

> I do not want to deny the reality of God, that God really exists. But it is not yet settled what the reality of God consists in. Gareth Moore (1988) *Believing in God* (T&T Clark), p. 101.

Moore's argument is that God is not a thing as other things are – he is 'no thing' – and hence his existence is of a quite different order from any 'thing'. But it is a huge gulf between his position and that of Cupitt, who could write no sentence like that above. Vardy appears to misunderstand Moore's notion of 'no thing'.

Religious Language – Verification and Meaning

2

Introduction

The most radical approach to problems of the meaning of religious terms would be simply to dismiss them as meaningless. Such would be the attitude of a group of philosophers known as the Vienna Circle, prominent in the two decades after the First World War, and taken seriously (some might argue too seriously) by later philosophers of religion, who have often felt the need to justify the meaning of not only their sentences but the very activity of their study.

The Vienna Circle (*Wiener Kreis*) was founded as a result of discussions in 1907 involving Otto Neurath, a sociologist, Hans Hahn, a mathematician and Philip Frank, a physicist. But real flourishing came after 1922 when Moritz Schlick (1882–1936) assumed leadership. He was Professor of the Philosophy of the Inductive Sciences, and the entire membership was very influenced by modern theories of Science. They were interested also in new developments in Logic as represented by Frege, Russell and Whitehead. Close attention was also given to the arguments of Ludwig von Wittgenstein (1889–1951). Some meetings were devoted to careful reading of his *Tractatus Logico-Philosophicus* of 1921. The Circle itself would last for little more than a decade. Many of its leaders were Jewish, some were Marxist, and with the rise of Nazism, sought to continue their careers elsewhere. Rudolf Carnap (1891–1970), a key figure, joined in 1926 but left in 1931, moving to the United States in 1935. Moritz Schlick was shot dead by an insane student while on his way to give a lecture. Otto Neurath (1882–1945) died in exile in Oxford. Each had, in various ways, shifted from the original 'pure' doctrine of the Circle – a doctrine referred to as Logical Positivism.

The Circle was past its peak when its ideas were brought to the attention of English readers by A. J. Ayer (Alfred Jules Ayer, later Sir Alfred, 1910–89), in the immensely influential *Language, Truth and Logic* of 1936. This book would become a huge best-seller, but, like Stephen Hawking's *A Brief History of Time*, perhaps more bought than read. Although clear to a philosopher, it is not always transparent to the general reader. Much attention focused on its treatment of ethics and religious beliefs. For all its faults, it remains the classic statement of Logical Positivism for the Anglophone world.

To understand the mission of Logical Positivism, we need to understand its philosophical antecedents. Nineteenth-century philosophy was dominated by the thought of G. W. F. Hegel (1770–1831) who argued for a view of the world in which everything ultimately forms part of a spiritual reality, the Absolute. He emphasized progress: in *The Philosophy of History*, he wrote: 'The history of the world is none other than the progress of the consciousness of freedom.' In detail, the theory was very complex. What worried Logical Positivists was that this was a philosophical attempt to state what the universe is like. Surely, it seemed to them, what the universe was like was a question to be investigated by scientists, using the tools of science, and not by philosophers constructing grand theories. It is difficult today to appreciate the extent of his influence but in the late nineteenth and early twentieth century, Hegelism was *the* dominant theory in European thought.

Probably the greatest blow to Hegelian optimism was the First World War – for many, it became impossible any longer to believe in inevitable progress after such carnage. The American Idealist philosopher, Josiah Royce (1855–1916), was emotionally broken by the torpedoing of the *Lusitania*, seeing it as disproving everything he had taught and believed: he died, a broken man, a few weeks later. Much of twentieth-century philosophy, whether in existentialism or the emphasis on logical analysis rather than the construction of systems was a reaction to the downfall of Hegelianism.

Against the Hegelians, the Logical Positivists offered no world view of their own. Indeed, they argued that it was no business of the philosopher to say anything at all about the world, and certainly not to indulge in Hegelian speculations. If you want information about the world, ask a scientist.

Verification Theory

If philosophers can say nothing about the world, of what may they speak? For the Logical Positivists, their role is to analyse the logical structure of sentences. This means that they determine whether a sentence is meaningful, that is, whether it is more than nonsense. The Logical Positivists conceived themselves as gatekeepers or certification officers for scientists, sorting out various propositions into those worthy of investigation and those empty of meaning. Into the latter category they would place most propositions of ethics, theology and aesthetics. It was not the philosopher's job to determine the truth of propositions, but rather whether they were sense or nonsense. To assert that the Matterhorn is the world's highest mountain is untrue, but it is not meaningless, because it is something the truth of which can be investigated by science.

Put simply, there are only two types of significant, that is, meaningful, propositions. First, there are tautologies, which are *a priori*, and true by definition. The sentence, 'A square has four sides' is necessarily true because the meaning of the term 'a square' necessarily includes having four sides. But, of course, this tells us nothing about the content of the world, only about the conventions of language. Tautologies include the whole of mathematics. Mathematics is a series of tautologies. Any sum is reducible to a straightforward and very simple tautology:

$$x = x$$

After all, when we say '7 + 5 = 12', '7 + 5' is only another way of writing '12'.[1]

The other type of significant sentence is the empirically verifiable proposition. This type of sentence is one that tells us something beyond itself and not simply about the meaning of its own terms. And the key to this is that it must entail an observation at some point, either directly (as in a statement about the desk at which I am writing) or indirectly (I cannot directly observe Julius Caesar, but I can observe the sense experiences of books, sounds etc. which lead to such knowledge of him as I may have).

What type of sentence does this rule out? Suppose I were to say that the universe doubled in size last night. It sounds like a significant – and hence meaningful – sentence, but further thought suggests that it is not, for there is no possible observation which could either prove or even make probable the truth of the sentence. If the universe doubled in size, we would notice no difference, because we would be twice the size, our furniture twice the size, our tape-measures twice the size and so on. Everything would look exactly the same as it does now. In practice, nothing would have changed.

Strong and Weak Verification

In the first edition of *Language, Truth and Logic*, Ayer distinguished between strong and weak verification:

> A proposition is said to be verifiable, in the strong sense of the term, if, and only if, its truth could be conclusively established in experience. But it is verifiable, in the weak sense, if it is possible for experience to render it probable. *Language, Truth and Logic*, p. 50.

Ayer goes on to point out that strong verification is impossible. We can never conclusively make any statement about the world, as our senses can be mistaken even about what we think is in front of us. I may be mistaken – for reasons we have seen – about whether my cat in front of me is really as I see her – I cannot get outside my mind to check my perception. Ayer points out that historical statements and the general conclusions of science would be unverifiable:

> It will be our contention that no proposition, other than a tautology, can possibly be more than a probable hypothesis. And if this is correct, the principle that a sentence can be factually significant only if it expresses what is conclusively verifiable is self-stultifying as a criterion of significance. For it leads to the conclusion that it is impossible to make a significant statement of fact at all. *Language, Truth and Logic*, p. 51.[2]

Instead, Ayer chose the weak form of verification outlined above. It is sufficient to state what observations would make the sentence probable. He gives the interesting example of a sentence stating that there are mountains on the far side of the moon. When he was writing, in 1935, no one had seen the far side of the moon and the technology capable of creating a rocket or spacecraft to make such an observation did not exist. But, it was possible to state what observations *would* make the statement probable, so it was possible to say that the sentence was significant – it was verifiable in principle.

It is perhaps worth noting that in the preface to second edition of *Language, Truth and Logic* (1946), Ayer amended his position. First, he argued that he made a pointless distinction, as, on his original account, he would have mentioned a class of propositions which was empty, as no empirical sentences were conclusively verifiable. Second, he argued that he now thought there was a small class of conclusively verifiable sentences, which he called 'basic statements'. These are perhaps difficult to understand. 'My cat is in front of me' is not a basic statement, because its truth value depends on the truth value of terms like 'cat' and 'me' which themselves rest on prior perceptions. Behind the sentence there seems to be something like 'there seems to be a cat-like appearance'. One cannot get behind a basic statement to something which justifies it: it is the basic justification of further observation sentences, such as the one about the cat. This takes us back to the problems of foundationalism mentioned in the last chapter, and there is disagreement between philosophers about what might count as a basic statement – even if they accept foundationalism. If in doubt, for this examination, don't worry about it!

Implications

The implications of Ayer's view are spelled out in robust terms in Chapter 6 of his book. He has already rejected metaphysics as meaningless, but the examples he gives are of transcendent metaphysics, especially those of Hegel and his followers. That is, he rejects as meaningless metaphysics which look outside immediate sense experience to God or the Absolute. These are not untrue, but are quite without meaning.

In Chapter 6, he rejects much of ethics, adopting emotivism, the belief that a sentence like, 'Cannibalism is wrong' simply *evinces* an emotion. It does not even *express* it. After all, a vegetarian may say 'cannibalism is right' if she finds herself among cannibals who think veggies are especially tasty when lightly grilled with herbs. . . . But she would not be expressing an emotion she actually felt.

He then disposes of aesthetics on similar grounds – to say this picture is beautiful states no facts but evinces an emotion about it.

He then turns to religious belief: he argues that ' "There exists a transcendent God" has no literal significance.'[3] It is important to notice here that Ayer is not simply arguing that theists are talking nonsense when they say 'God exists'. So too are atheists. If to say 'God exists' is meaningless, then to say 'God does not exist' is no less nonsense. Nonsense does not become sense by adding a negative: if 'floobbodybobodydoo' is nonsense, so too is '*not* floobbodybobodydoo'. Nor would Ayer accept agnosticism as meaningful: an agnostic thinks 'Is there a God?' is a real question which he cannot answer. For Ayer, the question itself is meaningless. Religious faith is nonsense, genuine religious experience impossible.

Reponses to Ayer

Language, Truth and Logic seemed to pose a major challenge to faith, not least because of the immense success of the book. Whether it succeeded as a challenge is another matter.

An obvious objection is that the verification principle itself is neither a tautology nor empirically verifiable. Its truth cannot be known by any process of observation. By its own rules, it seems itself to be meaningless.

Some Logical Positivists tried to argue for a class of protocol statements, that is, arguing that the verification principle was a statement of method. The problem with such an approach is that to invent another class of propositions inevitably undermines the original belief that there are only two types of significant proposition, tautologies and empirically verifiable propositions.

Another problem is that if we adopt the verification principle, we are committing ourselves to a form of foundationalism (see last chapter). We are assuming that there is an absolute foundation (which itself needs no further justification) from the viewpoint of which we can then go on to assert the rules for determining the meaningfulness of every other sentence. It is not clear that the statement that there are only two types of significant sentence can be justified other than by asserting it. The only permissible premises for justification would need themselves to be either tautologies or empirically justifiable sentences – and that would be circular, question-begging in the precise sense of the term.

Notice too the underlying assumptions of Logical Positivism. It takes as its assumption the paradigm (and, we shall suggest in the next chapter, a flawed paradigm) of science. It assumes that it is scientists and scientific statements which tell us about the world. Now, it is true that science gives us information about the world, and it would be foolish to deny that. But, is that the only informative language? Poetry reveals to us aspects of human experience which it alone can express. The language of poetry is not cognitive, any more than the language of music is, but it is, at its best, revelatory. A great work of art reveals to us new ways of looking at the world; but they are rarely straightforwardly cognitive or – in the Logical Positivist sense – verifiable scientific sentences.

At the heart of the Logical Positivist enterprise is the assumption that a verifiable sentence is a scientific one – remember that the purpose of the philosopher, according to this theory, is to determine what sentences it is worthwhile for scientists to investigate. But a Shakespeare sonnet is not a scientific hypothesis. It would be a bold literary critic who thought the latter without meaning. To reduce sentences to two classes – the meaningful, and hence open to scientific investigation, or the meaningless, – creates problems. It is not a self-evident truth that the many uses of sentences can be so easily reduced to just two classes.

It is the argument of many philosophers of religion that religious sentences are of a quite different order. Vincent Brümmer, the distinguished South African/Dutch[4] theologian and philosopher has recently argued that to treat the sentences of faith as if they were scientific sentences – as the verification theory does – is to commit an error of understanding. He, like D. Z. Phillips before him, believes that we make the error of treating religious sentences in terms set by Enlightenment thinkers, such as Hume, (and, more recently, Dawkins) seeing them as having the character of failed scientific sentences. This is an error: just as the methods of scientific analysis are inappropriate to poetry, so they are to the experience and utterances of faith. Professor Brümmer comments, writing of the atheism of Flew and Dawkins:

> The success of science has had the effect that for many of us today the search for knowledge has become the paradigmatic model for all our thinking. Today many of us intuitively assume that *all* thinking is aimed at extending our knowledge, that human beings are mere knowing subjects and that reality is merely the object of knowledge. The effect of this mindset for the way religious faith is understood has been disastrous. Vincent Brümmer: *What Are We Doing When We Pray* (Revised and Expanded Edition), Ashgate, 2008, pp. 141–2.

Brümmer argues that we have, in modern times, tended to assume that if something is not scientific or measurable that it is somehow not very significant. But even to think that is to make an assumption we cannot justify: it is not self-evidently true and it is difficult to see what could be evidence to demonstrate that the modern view is correct.

There are, however, good grounds for arguing – as we shall see in the next chapter – that the Logical Positivists presuppose a deeply flawed vision of science.

STRETCH AND CHALLENGE

A very unconvincing argument against Ayer is made by Richard Swinburne in *The Coherence of Theism*. He gives a much-quoted example of a sentence which he holds to be unverifiable but nevertheless meaningful:

> Some of the toys which to all appearance stay in the toy cupboard while people are asleep and no one is watching actually get up and dance in the middle of the night and then go back to the cupboard, leaving no traces of their activity. Richard Swinburne: *The Coherence of Theism*, (Revised edition, 1993), p. 28.

This example is much more problematic than Swinburne seems to realise. First, it obviously does not satisfy the weak verification principle (assuming we presume the non-existence of CCTV cameras!).

But, it does not follow that the weak verification principle fails as a criterion for genuinely factual statements, because we would need to demonstrate that this sentence is a genuinely factual statement by means *other than* the verification principle. Think about this for a moment. If it is not meaningful in terms of the verification principle, then it must be meaningful in terms of something else. Swinburne needs to tell us what that alternative might be. The truth of the sentence cannot be empirically grounded, because we cannot state any observations which would enable us to say we are justified in holding that this is a genuinely factual sentence.

Swinburne appeals to the fact that we *understand* the sentence because we understand all the words contained in it. The understanding of the words is based on our ability to make conceptions of things, such as toys, feelings and so on. That understanding is based on the world as we conceptualise it, and it is on the basis of our conceptualization that we understand the meaning of every word in the sentence about toys. If we can understand the meaning of each word, because we have learned the meaning of that word, we can make some sense of a sentence made up of words that we can understand. But it does not follow that *because* each word is understood, that because of how we formulate our concepts, a sentence made up entirely of words we can understand, is itself, as a sentence, coherent or genuinely factual. 'We are sitting in the train' has a factual possibility and coherence quite different from: 'The train is sitting in us', even though we understand every element of the sentence. 'I understand the meaning of all the words in a sentence' is not identical with 'That sentence is genuinely factual'. I understand the words in a sentence about the universe doubling in size at midnight, but it is not, simply because I understand each of the words, necessarily a genuinely factual sentence. When Ayer looks at a sentence such as 'God exists' he is not denying that we can have some understanding of the words, but that the sentence as a whole is unverifiable.

In any case, even if Swinburne were right that the sentence about the cupboard is meaningful, it would not follow that sentences about God were meaningful, because they are not of the same kind as sentences about toys.

Believers, such as D. Z. Phillips would argue that a sentence such as 'God creates and sustains the earth' is a sentence of a quite different type from 'water is made of hydrogen and oxygen.' To be sure, the first sentence looks a bit like the second in structure, but it is very different. God is not a creator in the same sense as a potter is the creator of the clay jug, nor would he be a thing like an element such as hydrogen. Whatever God's existence may be, it would be nothing like anything in the universe. Phillips always insisted that the search for God is a *religious* rather than a scientific quest. Such an approach opens the question of what it means to be a religious quest, but, whatever the answer to that may be, the logic of the quest would be different.

(This point is applicable against a thinker such as Dawkins, who argues that God fails as a scientific hypothesis: to say that God made the world is to say something different from ' "The Big Bang" made the world'. The second sentence is a genuinely scientific sentence where 'made' refers to processes which are in principle open to scientific investigation, because they would be something like other scientifically known processes. But God's making of the world would be nothing like that, because God would not be like any known – or knowable – scientific process.)

Think of this another way. When we are on a scientific quest, we understand both the subject and object terms in a sentence. Take, for example, the sentences:

1. I am seeking the Loch Ness Monster.
2. Scientists are looking for the cure for cancer.

In both cases, we understand the whole sentence, both the subject ('I', 'Scientists') *and* the object, ('the Loch Ness Monster', 'the cure for cancer'). We know very well the conditions and tests which would enable us to say 'I have found the monster.' We can state with great precision what would convince those who believe the monster to be a consequence of an over-active imagination that they were wrong. I do not know what the cure for cancer would be, but I know exactly what clinical results would follow if it were ever found.

But, consider this sentence:

I am seeking God.

The sentence looks identical in structure to the sentences about the cure for cancer and the Loch Ness Monster, but it is very different. I cannot define the object term, 'God', in that way. I cannot tell you the tests which would demonstrate that I had indeed found God, because I do not know what the God is that I seek. The term 'God' represents something of a quite different and incomprehensible (in the sense of surpassing human understanding) order. One cannot say 'kind', for there would be nothing quite like God. It makes no sense to say that God is this sort of thing or that sort of thing. But it does not follow that because I cannot understand a given term in a sentence that the sentence is, in itself, meaningless, any more than that I know the meaning of all the words entails the factual possibility of the sentence as a whole.

Swinburne's sentence about the toys in the cupboard is quite unlike any sentence in which 'God' is a term. In Swinburne's case, I can understand every name in the sentence because I am acquainted with the concept from other sense experiences. I know what a toy is, what a cupboard is, from other contexts. That is why the words in the sentence have meaning for me. But 'God' is not the object of a sense experience in any ordinary way, nor by any way achievable by the methods of science – there is no Godometer to measure him by. So, the meaning of 'God' is not a measurable or quantifiable concept any more than it is based on normal sense experience. We cannot go from an assumption that a statement about toys in a cupboard is meaningful to assume that a sentence about God is meaningful in the same way.

Exercise and Examination Advice

Make a list of the following terms in your notes and make sure you research them until you have a clear understanding of what each means:

Vienna Circle

Logical Positivism

Verification Principle

Strong Verification

Weak Verification

Tautology

A priori

Untrue

Meaningless

You should also be able to demonstrate a good understanding of the views of writers such as:

The Vienna Circle

A. J. Ayer

Anthony Flew

As can be seen from this chapter, many other writers have contributed to this debate and you should, along with your teachers, research some of their views. However, examiners cannot expect you to quote from philosophers who are not on the specification and they will not ask specific questions about philosophers not listed on the said specification. That said, the more research you do and the wider your understanding is developed, the better your answers will be. Hegel's writings are very complex and no one is expecting you to produce a discourse on the Hegelian dialectic; however, understanding that the Logical Positivists did not appear in a vacuum is one important way of approaching this issue. The limits of their conclusions, for example, can be found in the very exercise they set themselves.

As we indicated a great deal in the AS book, the key when it comes to responding to examination questions, is to tailor your answer to the specific question in front of you. I have seen an ethics answer, for example, where the candidate had a liking for the writings of Nietzsche and produced an excellent response from his philosophical views which scored full marks even though Nietzsche was not on the specification and nowhere to be seen in the mark scheme. The key was that the candidate took writing that she understood well and applied it relevantly and critically to the question which had been set.

Now, using the information above, and adding your own research and reflection, try answering the following:

To what extent were the Logical Positivists successful in arguing that all religious language is meaningless? (35)

Notes

1. This point is explained with great clarity by Ayer in Chapter 4 of *Language, Truth and Logic*, 'The *A Priori*'. References throughout this text are to the 1971 Penguin edition. Later editions move Ayer's second edition preface to the back, without altering all the footnote references.
2. Too many textbooks get this point wrong, which is odd, as Ayer is so unambiguous.
3. *Language, Truth and Logic*, p. 158.
4. South African born, he was educated at Stellenbosch, Harvard, Utrecht and Oxford, and was invited to be Professor in the Philosophy of Religion at Utrecht, a post he held for 30 years. He has dual nationality.

Religious Language – The Falsification Debate 3

Introduction

Logical Positivism has, as we have seen, been much criticized. Its claim to determine the distinction between meaningful sentences and others was much criticized. Dorothy Emmet (1904–2000) made a robust defence of metaphysics in *The Nature of Metaphysical Thinking*, first published in 1945.[1] Younger philosophers, such as Anthony Flew (1923–), also found much wanting in the assumptions of verification theory.

But the most significant opponent of Logical Positivism was Karl Raimund Popper (1902–94). He was born in Austria, and was educated at the University of Vienna, where he received his PhD in 1928. After the rise of Nazism, he emigrated to New Zealand, where he lectured for a decade before moving to London as Professor in Logic and Scientific Method at the London School of Economics. He was knighted in 1965, by which time he had been fully recognized as perhaps the most significant figure in the Philosophy of Science, as well as a major contributor to political thought.

His seminal *The Open Society and Its Enemies* had been written in New Zealand. Popper is always worth reading – the clarity and elegance of his English style provide a model of good writing.

While studying in Vienna, he became acquainted with – and indeed, friendly with – many of the leading figures in the Vienna Circle. But because of his disagreement with the conclusions of Logical Positivism, he was never invited to their meetings. Otto Neurath described Popper as 'The Official Opposition.' His approach to science, and his opposition to the principle of verification, were set out in *Logik der Forschung* of 1934 (translated as *The Logic of Scientific Discovery*, 1959).

Falsification

Popper's opposition to verification theory was based on the assumption of the Vienna Circle that what mattered was to be able to prove scientific propositions true. Popper pointed out that if we believe that science is about proving our views to be true, we would make no progress at all. We would also have the wrong mindset when conducting experiments.

When conducting experiments, we should not look to verify theories, but to falsify them. Only in that way does science progress – we recognize, through continual criticism, weaknesses in our existing theories, discard them, and try to produce better ones. If we conducted all our experiments on the assumption that they would prove our theories true, we would want to explain away anomalies and exceptions. But it is the anomalies and exceptions which tell us that there is something wrong with our original theory. Popper, who was sometimes rather peppery in manner, would become cross with those who took the lazy view that it is the exception that proves the rule: he would point out that it is the exception which *disproves* the rule.

Thus, for Popper, the key activity is that of *falsification*. The mark of a genuinely scientific statement is that it is possible to state what would falsify it.

Anthony Flew explains the point very clearly:

> Popper's contention was ... that, whereas no theory and no proposition may be accounted scientific even when it is known to be false, no theory and no proposition can be properly presented as even a possible contribution to science unless its proponents are prepared to specify what would have to happen, or to have happened, for it to be falsified; that is, shown to be false.
> Anthony Flew: *An Introduction to Western Philosophy*, revised edition, Thames and Hudson, 1989, p. 482.

So the method of science is not of verification but of falsification. Real science is highly falsifiable, for, if it were not, then it would not be informative.

Suppose I were a meteorologist who wanted never to be caught out with a wrong forecast. My forecast is: 'It will rain, somewhere, sometime.' That is very likely to be true, but it does not tell me whether I will need my umbrella tomorrow. A truly useful forecast would be: 'It will be raining at 9.00 in Brighton tomorrow.' That forecast is much more informative – and much more likely to be wrong, because it could be wrong in so many details – time, place and so on. If we give more information, our theories become more improbable – but that is why they are valuable. As Popper often remarked, high probability does not count in favour of a theory: its high probability means it is not very informative.

A key advantage of falsifiability is, according to Popper, that some statements can be conclusively falsified when they cannot be conclusively verified. To say all giraffes have long necks would be at best highly probable – it could only be verified by seeing every possible giraffe, past, present and future. Just because every giraffe so far noted has had a long neck, it does not follow every giraffe will do so. But, the moment I have found just one short-necked giraffe, I have falsified the original hypothesis. The man who thought all adult swans were white was disproven by the discovery of the first Australian black swan.

It is essential to note that falsifiability is not a criterion to determine whether something is meaningful or not, only whether it has the status of a scientific assertion. As Flew says:

> . . . . Popper proposed his Falsification Principle. Unlike the Verification Principle of the Logical Positivists, this was put forward as *a criterion not of meaning but of scientific status*.*ibid*: p. 482 [our italics].

As Popper pointed out, much of our science originated in unfalsifiable myth, neither would he deny meaning to utterances such as prayer, ethical commands or poetry: his point was that they were not science. He attacked Marxism and psychiatry as unscientific, but it does not follow that they have no meaning.

Anthony Flew and the *University* Debate

The most discussed – and anthologized – use of falsification in relation to religion was the *University* debate, 'Theology and Falsification', which involved Anthony Flew, Basil Mitchell and R. M. Hare. The entire debate is very brief and non-technical and should be read by any serious student of the subject.

Flew begins by referring to John Wisdom's parable of the gardener, from his article 'Gods'. The story is simple. Two explorers come upon a clearing in the jungle. Some parts look tended, others do not. In Wisdom's original parable, he is making the point that the world is rather like that. In the original, one man takes the view there is a gardener who comes to tend the ground, while the other thinks there is not. Neither can find the gardener, neither experiences anything the other does not, yet their belief about the clearing is very different.

Flew draws a slightly different conclusion. He asks what is the difference between the apparently invisible, intangible, scentless, soundless gardener and no gardener at all? It looks as if what seemed a genuinely scientific hypothesis, that a gardener comes to the clearing, is actually not a genuinely scientific hypothesis because the believer in the gardener does not accept falsification – he claims ever deeper invisibility, but still believes in the gardener.

Flew applies the question to theological assertions:

> And in this, it seems to me, lies the peculiar danger, the endemic evil, of theological utterance. Take such utterances as 'God has a plan', 'God created the world', 'God love us as a father loves his children'. They look at first sight very much like assertions, vast cosmological assertions. Of course, this is no sure sign that they either are, or are intended to be, assertions. But let us confine ourselves to the cases where those who utter such sentences intend them to express assertions.[2]

Notice that the question is about the status of the sentences, as genuine assertions. Flew goes on to say that for an assertion to be genuine, it must be falsifiable: 'if there is nothing which a putative assertion denies then there is nothing which it asserts either: and so it is not really an assertion.'[3]

He notes that it sometimes seems that for the believer nothing appears to falsify his belief. If the problem of evil is cited as denying God's love, believers resort to sayings such as 'God's love surpasses understanding' or 'God's love is not merely human'. As a consequence, Flew issues this challenge:

> Just what would have to happen not merely (morally and wrongly) to tempt but also (logically and rightly) to entitle us to say 'God does not love us' or even 'God does not exist'? I therefore put to the succeeding symposiasts the simple central questions, 'What would have to occur or to have occurred to constitute for you a disproof of the love of, or of the existence of God?'[4]

R. M. Hare and *bliks*

Hare's response is that Flew is right on his own ground, arguing instead that religious beliefs are what he calls 'bliks'. He gives the case of an insane university student who believes all the university dons are out to kill him. No evidence will dissuade him – if presented with a gentle and kindly don, he will see this as evidence only of the diabolical cunning of a profession trying to engender in him a false sense of security. Hare notes that while the lunatic's view can neither be proven nor disproven, it profoundly alters the lunatic's life. He argues:

Let us call that in which we differ from this lunatic, our respective *bliks*. He has an insane *blik* about dons; we have a sane one. It is important to realize that we have a sane one, not no *blik* at all; for there must be two sides to any argument – if he has a wrong *blik*, then those who are right about dons must have a right one.[5]

Hare argues that we all have *bliks* and they profoundly affect our lives. Hare gives the example of driving a car – we assume that the structure we drive will remain solid while we do so: we do not and cannot *know* this, and can neither prove nor disprove it.

Hare argues that the concept of *blik* shows what we are doing when we make a religious statement. It is not merely a sort of explanation of the world, but is completely life-changing, even though unfalsifiable. It is a matter of the very deepest concern.

Hare's position is superficially convincing, but is vulnerable. Flew argues that Hare's view is at odds with Christian belief and practice. He argues that the intention of the believer is to say something about the cosmos:

Religious utterances may indeed express false or even bogus assertions: but I simply do not believe that they are not both intended and interpreted to be or at any rate to presuppose assertions, at least in the context of religious practice.[6]

No less potent is the criticism of John Hick, who argues:

We want to distinguish, in Hare's terminology, between right and wrong *bliks*. . . . Hare assumes that one can make this distinction; for he identifies one *blik* as sane and the contrary *blik* as insane. But there seems to be an inconsistency in his position here, for a discrimination between sane (= right) and insane (= wrong) *bliks* is ruled out by his insistence that *bliks* are unverifiable and unfalsifiable. If experience can never yield either confirmation or disconfirmation of religious *bliks*, there is no basis for speaking of them as being right or wrong, appropriate or inappropriate, sane or insane.[7]

Basil Mitchell and the Partisan

Basil Mitchell (1917–) responded to Flew in a more interesting, and perhaps more successful, way. Unlike Hare, he wanted to maintain that religious statements are genuinely factual though not straightforwardly falsifiable. He tells his own parable. This would have been readily understandable in the immediate post-war years when the debate took place, but today it possibly requires a word or two of explanation.

When the Resistance was created in occupied countries like France, during the Second World War, secrecy was essential. The Gestapo would use torture to gain information to round up other members of the Resistance. To minimize casualties, remembering that even the strongest will crack under torture, the Resistance organized itself into small cells, of perhaps a dozen or so men and women. Ideally, only one member of the cell would know the identity of one member of the next cell in the chain. The idea was that if one cell member were caught and tortured, the Gestapo could not just roll up the entire Resistance network.

Mitchell's parable talks of the resistance fighter who meets a stranger who impresses him deeply. They spend a night in conversation, during which the Stranger claims to be the head of the entire Resistance. The fighter believes him, but is warned by the Stranger that his faith will be sorely tested – that at times he will find the man he trusted apparently working with the enemy. Despite this, and although they never again share such a conversation, the partisan persists in his belief that the Stranger is who he claims to be. He maintains his belief even when he sees the Stranger in the uniform of the occupying force.

Mitchell's point is that the partisan does not deny that there is strong evidence against his belief that the Stranger is who he claims to be. Mitchell argues that to remain sane, the partisan *must accept* the reality of the evidence against his belief. If he does not, he is 'guilty of a failure of faith as well as logic.'[8] If he does not accept that there is strong evidence against the belief in a loving God, then the believer is guilty of self delusion: if the believer does not accept the strength of the argument, his beliefs become '. . . vacuous formulae (expressing, perhaps, a desire for reassurance) to which experience makes no difference and which make no difference to life'.[9]

But Mitchell does not argue that the believer just has faith – he has reason for his faith, which is a belief in the personal character of the Stranger. Mitchell says:

> It is here that my parable differs from Hare's. The partisan admits that many things may and do count against his belief: whereas Hare's lunatic who has a *blik* about dons doesn't admit that anything counts against his *blik*. Nothing *can* count against *bliks*. Also the partisan has a reason for having in the first instance committed himself, viz. the character of the Stranger; whereas the lunatic has no reason for his *blik* about dons – because, of course, you can't have reasons for *bliks*.[10]

John Hick has further glossed Mitchell's parable in two important ways, which connect with his own parable. Hick argues:

- Presumably the Stranger himself knows whether he is telling the truth, even though the partisan is not in a position to make the judgement.
- When the war is over the truth will emerge. Either the Stranger will be greeted as a great hero, smothered with medals, or led away and (one assumes) shot as a traitor.

Hick uses these considerations to develop his own response to both falsification and verification.

John Hick and Eschatological Verification

Hick, in arguments which can be found in slightly different forms in different places,[11] argued that Christianity has certain specific afterlife beliefs which mean that one can at least meet the conditions of weak verification. Christians who believe in an afterlife can state what experiences would render their beliefs probable. (Remember, as with Ayer's example of the mountains on the far side of the moon, that one has only state what position one would need to be in to make the observation possible). Suppose I believe that when I die I will see Christ in heaven. Suppose further that I die, know I have died, and experience the things I have always believed I would experience. In those circumstances I can verify my original belief and say I was right all along.

The problem with this solution is that it is, to use Hick's term, an asymmetrical solution to problems raised by verification and falsification. As Hick says:

> The hypothesis of continued existence after bodily death provides ... [an] ... instance of a proposition *which is verifiable if true but not falsifiable if false* [our italics]. This hypothesis entails a prediction that one will, after the date of one's bodily death, have conscious experiences, including the experience of remembering that death. This is a prediction that will be verified in one's own experience if it is true but that cannot be falsified if it is false. That is to say, it can be false, but *that* it is false can never be a fact that anyone has experientially verified.[12]

Hick seems to equate falsification with verification theory. This is an error because although he has demonstrated very clearly how certain specifically Christian beliefs might satisfy the demands of weak verification, and are thus meaningful, he has failed to demonstrate against the claims of falsification theory that Christian claims are genuinely falsifiable propositions. Indeed, it seems to be a consequence of his argument that the claims of faith are not scientific hypotheses at all.

Conclusion

To reach such a position might not be such a problem for the believer if she argues that religious belief is not a scientific belief at all. Clearly, whatever kinds of explanations might constitute understanding, a religious explanation does not have the character of a scientific explanation in any ordinary sense. God is not a cause in the way a collision of elements is a cause. We are dealing with questions of a different type. The difficulty is in determining what that type might be. And that is where the problems begin. I can relate my description of physical causes to other examples of physical causes, developing analogies, demonstrating how this type of cause is the same as that, and where it is different (Aristotle's notion of classification *per genus et per differentia*). But it is that which I cannot do with sentences about God – there is nothing he is like, no parallel or analogy which covers the case adequately.

But, as John Cottingham has argued:[13]

> It is precisely because the great truths of religion are held to be in part a mystery, beyond the direct comprehension of the human mind, that an attempt to grasp them head on via the tools of logical analysis is, in a certain sense, to evade them. A different strategy, the strategy of involvement, the strategy of praxis, is required by the nature of the material.

In similar vein, Vincent Brummer argues:

> *Metaphysical claims* about the existence and nature of God are obviously not open to empirical verification or falsification since God is not an empirically observable object . . . In the light of faith we could experience the world as an expression of the grace of God or as the context in which we are called to do God's will, but not as an experience of God as such.[14]

But it does not follow from these considerations that we can simply dismiss statements about God as non-cognitive utterance. It remains possible to ask whether they are true or false. To say that religious sentences are not reducible to scientific assertions is a wholly separate question from whether they are true or false.

Exercise and Examination Advice

Make a list of the following terms in your notes and make sure you research them until you have a clear understanding of what each means:

Logical Positivism (reacquaint yourself with the term)

Falsification

Scientific propositions

Anomalies

Scientific hypothesis

Putative assertions

Bliks

Eschatological verification

You should also be able to demonstrate a good understanding of the views of writers such as:

Anthony Flew

As we have said before, questions can only be set on writers named in the specification. However it would be difficult, if not impossible, to understand this part of the debate fully if you have not also read:

Popper

Mitchell

Hare

Hick

As has been mentioned earlier in the chapter, the Symposium itself is only a few pages long and it is worth the effort to read through it carefully. As we suggested at AS, it may be worth trying to get different groups in the class to take on the role of arguing for particular parts of the published debate, ignoring the others views until they have presented their own side and then see where the debate goes.

Alternatively a class may want to split into groups to explore the question of whether or not a purely scientific approach can explain the world or whether a purely religious approach can explain the world, again firmly researching and presenting one side of the argument before listening to the other and then taking the debate on in their own directions.

You could then try to answer the following question:

Critically assess the argument that believers never permit their views to be treated as science. (35)

Notes

1. Macmillan, subsequently several times reissued.
2. Anthony Flew et al. (1955) 'Theology and Falsification', *New Essays in Philosophical Theology*, eds. Anthony Flew and Alisdair MacIntyre (SCM), p. 97.
3. *Ibid.*, p. 98.
4. *Ibid.*, p. 99.
5. *Ibid.*, p. 100.
6. *Ibid.*, p. 108.
7. John Hick: *Philosophy of Religion*, 2nd Edition, Prentice Hall, 1973, pp. 88–9.
8. Anthony Flew et al. (1955) 'Theology and Falsification', *New Essays in Philosophical Theology*, eds. Anthony Flew and Alisdair MacIntyre (SCM), p. 105
9. *Ibid.*, p. 105.
10. *Ibid.*, p. 105.
11. Initially in his essay 'Theology and Verification', *Theology Today*, XVII, No. 1, April 1960, further developed in *Faith and Knowledge*, Macmillan 1967 as Chapter 8, and found also in his *Philosophy of Religion*.
12. John Hick (1973) *Philosophy of Religion* (2nd Edition, Prentice Hall), p. 91.
13. John Cottingham (2005) *The Spiritual Dimension* (Cambridge), p. 12.
14. Vincent Brümmer (2008) *What Are We Doing When We Pray?* (2nd edition, Ashgate), p. 171.

Religious Language – *Via Negativa,* Analogy, Symbol and Myth `4`

Introduction

We have so far considered whether religious language can be meaningful or whether it involves genuinely scientific hypotheses. A second, and separate, question is what that religious language might mean, assuming that it is in some sense meaningful but that it cannot wholly capture a God who is beyond the ability of the human mind to conceive.

In this chapter we shall consider various attempts to attribute meaning to God.

Via Negativa (The Apophatic Way)

Perhaps the most radical – if the most understandable – way is to deny that we can say anything about God at all. We can say what God is not – not at all what he is. So, for example, we could say God is not a goldfish, not temporal, not mortal, not ignorant and so on. What we cannot do is to say the God *is* timeless, all-knowing and so on, because we cannot begin to comprehend what these terms mean in relation to God. We use them only with human understanding as human words. As a result, they cannot be used with any significant meaning. In an important sense, this view taps into a deep religious instinct. In Judaism, the very name of God is not fully articulated, in Islam God is never portrayed and the deepest perception of the great mystics is the unfathomable nature of God.

The *apophatic* way (the term *apophatic*, a Greek neologism, suggests a collapse of language in the face of the Infinite) of dealing with theology is found especially in Eastern Christian thought, with elements appearing in the work of both Origen (185–254) and Clement of Alexandria (d. c.215). The same trend in the attempt to talk about God is found in the neo-Platonists, especially Proclus (410–85). In late Arianism, Eunomius (d. c.395) treated God as directly knowable, but Basil the Great (330–79) and Gregory of Nyassa (c.332–c.398) pointed to the human inability to know the essence of God. If we cannot know the mind and essence of an ant, we can never begin to understand God. According to Evagrius Ponticus (345–99), the highest understanding is 'pure prayer' a union with God without words or images, a bare awareness of something beyond anything created.

Early in the sixth century, Pseudo-Dionysius (Dionysius the Areopagite, *fl.* 500) made a distinction between 'cataphatic' (*via positiva*) and 'apophatic 'theology (*via negativa*). In the former, we contemplate God as he is in relation to the world, using the divine names like 'The Good', 'Light of the World', 'Life' and so on. These do give us real knowledge of God, but it is provisional knowledge, for God lies far beyond those names. If God is Light, he is far beyond that feeble attempt to capture him. The knowledge of God lies beyond the world. To move to the apophatic way, the *via negativa*, is to move beyond – to 'the divine darkness' which lies beyond any concept.

This view was strongest in the Eastern Church, but it was found also in Western Christianity, notably in the work of John Scotus Eriugena (c.810–c.877). He was an Irish monk, who lived most of his later life in France. Apart from his own important philosophical works, he translated significant parts of the works of the Pseudo-Dionysius, and the influence can be seen strongly in his own treatment of God.

The *via negativa* was adopted by the medieval Jewish philosopher, Moses Maimonides (1135–1204). St Thomas Aquinas had a profound knowledge of Maimonides' work, but saw *via negativa* as a prelude to understanding God. After all, to say God is not ignorant or not limited by time surely tells us *something* about God even if we cannot know what that something may be. Even to say that God is not a goldfish gives us a tiny piece of positive information though no deep insight into the nature of God.

Some Christian thinkers have been deeply worried about some aspects of the apophatic way. W. R. Inge (1860–1954), famous for his long service as Dean of St Paul's Cathedral, worried that to deny God his descriptions was to lead to annihilation of God and self. A concern for many theologians is that to strip God of his descriptions, because our descriptions are based on finite experience, is to lose the essential link between God and the world. Christian orthodoxy insists on God's involvement in the world, in a God who so loved the world that he gave his only son for its sake. The opposition to Gnostic heresies such as Manichaeanism rested precisely on the insistence that matter was of God and in no sense a denial of God. More modern Christian thinkers, notably G. K. Chesterton (1874–1936) and Pierre Teilhard de Chardin (1881–1955), who spoke of the 'divinisation of matter', insisted on finding God in and through the earth, through the material, which was all part of his divine plan of salvation. The fear was that the *via negativa* placed God too far beyond human life and the human world.

Perhaps a more balanced approach would be to argue that we need both *via negativa* and *via positiva*. The former stands as a constant reminder not to anthropomorphize God, the latter, perhaps, tells us that if we are to say anything at all, that utterance needs some content, however tentative, to express anything at all.

It was in response to the need to find some balance between the unknown, incomprehensible God of *via negativa* and the religious need to say something positive, that Aquinas developed the Doctrine of Analogy.

Analogy

St Thomas Aquinas developed the Doctrine of Analogy, but he was not the only one to recognize that language involves an approximation of the reality which it describes. Supporters of the apophatic way argue that language is wholly inadequate to describe God. Aquinas attempts to hold together two points: that human language is indeed inadequate to express the divine, but that we do not have to assume from that, that it is saying nothing.

Aquinas argued that there are three types of significant language:

- univocal
- equivocal
- analogical

Univocal language is when a word or phrase is used in the same way in two different sentences. To say: 'My cat is black', 'Your cat is ginger' is to use the word 'cat' in the same way in two sentences – in each case referring to a domestic feline. The meaning is the same. Religious language is clearly not like that – we do not use words about God in the way we use them about ourselves: to do so would be to anthropomorphize him.

On the other hand, we are not using language equivocally. Consider the sentences: 'There is a bat in the belfry', 'I have bought a new bat for cricket.' The term 'bat' means something totally different in each sentence, and although the terms are the same, they are to be understood wholly differently. For Aquinas, religious language is not like that. If any sentence about God had a wholly different meaning from any other usage, then we would not have religious language but silence.

But, he argues, we do mean something if we say, 'God is Love' or 'God is perfectly just.' There is something to be said. We are saying that there is enough in human behaviour to transfer some of the meaning to God without emptying the human concept entirely of meaning.

Aquinas recognized two types of analogy: *attribution* and *proportion*.

God is creator of the universe and everything ultimately comes from him. Now, we know that from a work of art, even if we know nothing of the artist, we can deduce something about him from the artefact – he was a good colourist, used broad brush-strokes, etc. But he is nothing like the work of art, even though we can say limited things about him from the picture. Aquinas gives a different and rather graphic example. From the appearance of a bull's urine, an expert can tell whether the bull is healthy – but it does not follow that the bull is just like a puddle of his urine. Nevertheless, the inference of health is justifiable. If the earth is God's handiwork, then we can attribute certain characteristics to him.

Analogy of proportion is based on the notion that if something is true of a given person then it is possible to be more true of another. If you are good, but your friend better at athletics, then we can say that she is twice or three times better than you are. In the same way, if you are just, we can say that God is proportionately more just than you are. The problem, of course, is that God is infinitely more just than you are: because we know he is many times more just, it does not follow that we can conceive of the extent of that goodness or justice.

Baron von Hügel (1852–1925), despite his name a British-based Roman Catholic theologian, tried to clarify the point:

> The source and object of religion, if religion be true and its object . . . real, *cannot*, indeed, *by any possibility, be as clear to me even as I am to my dog*. . . . in the case of religion . . . we apprehend and affirm realities indefinitely superior in quality and amount of reality to ourselves, and which, nevertheless (or rather, just because of this), anticipate, penetrate, and sustain us with a quite unpicturable intimacy. The obscurity of my life to my dog must . . . be greatly exceeded by the obscurity of the life of God to me. Indeed the obscurity of plant life – so obscure for my mind, because so indefinitely

inferior and poorer than is my human life – must be greatly exceeded by the dimness, for my human life, of God – of His reality and life, so different and superior, so unspeakably more rich and alive, than is, or can ever be, my own life and reality.[1]

When we speak of God, we are saying that God's Love, or whatever quality it is, is something like that in humans. There is enough in common that permits us to use the term.

The purpose of the Doctrine of Analogy is not to tell us precisely what the terms we are using about God actually *mean*, for that we cannot know. But it does permit us to say *something* positive, limited though it will indeed be. The understanding will always be very limited. That is why Aquinas is so insistent on the need for such careful awareness of what we are doing when we talk of God: he insists on the ultimate incomprehensibility of God. What analogy does is to tell us not what the words mean but what we are doing when we are talking about God: it is a continual reminder of both the limits of language and the danger of anthropomorphism.

An interesting perspective on analogy is found in the work of John McQuarrie (1919–2007), who argues:

the way of analogy is the one that has the most positive content. It is not, of course, a literal or direct way of talking about God, and yet it is a way that seems to give us assurance that our talk is not just empty, and that it does somehow impinge upon God and give us some insight into the mystery of Being. Analogy makes possible that language of scripture and liturgy that is at the heart of the Christian religion. . . . Unless we can say that it is meaningful, I think honest people would want to get rid of the whole business.[2]

Ian Ramsey and Analogy

Ian Ramsey (1915–72), who was Bishop of Durham and author of *Religious Language*,[3] was very conscious that any use of religious language was always odd, and speculated that there must be something in language that we might use to make sense of God. He developed two key notions – the *disclosure situation* and *qualified models*.

A *disclosure situation* occurs when we see through and beyond the reality in front of us. To use a favourite example of Ramsey, a geometer draws a regular polygon, redrawing it with additional sides – sixteen, fifty sides on so on. At a certain point we see it suddenly *as* a circle, even though close examination would show it to be made up of many tiny straight lines. We would see beyond the lines to the circle that lies beyond its literal shape. It is that moving beyond which happens when we use religious language. The language we use is the *qualified model*. Suppose we say that 'God is First Cause'. When we say 'Cause' we mean this is a *model*, for God would not be a cause in any sense that we might understand the term from Physics or Chemistry or Biology: the 'Cause' is simply something like 'cause' in the normal sense. And the use of 'First' brings home the very special use of 'Cause' – it qualifies the notion to show both that it is a model and that the term is being used in a very special sense.

Two thoughts arise. It is not clear that we are being offered here anything which is not part of Aquinas' notion of analogy. The value of Ramsey lies in his explanation and clarification of an essentially old idea – it is not obviously a new one. Second, Karl Barth (1886–1968) argues that Ramsey's approach, and indeed, analogy in general, is mistaken because we cannot approach God through means of language based on our existing experience: we need revelation:

> What we can represent to ourselves lies in the sphere of our own existence, and of existence generally, as distinct from God. If we do know about God as Creator, it is neither wholly nor partially because we have a prior knowledge of something that resembles creation. It is only because it has been given to us by God's revelation to know him. . . . Karl Barth: *Church Dogmatics*, 'The Doctrine of God', Vol II/I, pp. 76–7.[4]

If Barth is right, analogy would fail, but so too would any other attempt to give meaning to God-talk. If God's revelations are expressible, they are expressible in human language as the only one we might understand. If we cannot understand God in our language, he would need that language to express himself to us. If God has taught us that he is First Cause, then there is something that term expresses.

Symbol

Paul Tillich (1886–1965) developed an interesting theory of religious language as symbolic. The question about this is whether this adds anything significant to analogy or whether it is simply a different perspective on the same issue.

Tillich distinguishes between a *sign* and a *symbol*. A sign is merely conventional, in the way a road sign may indicate a hazard, or a bend ahead, or the way a pointing finger may indicate the direction we should follow to find the lavatory or the exit.

If a sign is merely a matter of convention, then a *symbol* points towards something *and* participates in that to which it points. Consider the Stars-and-Stripes as a flag. Certainly it is a sign which stands for part of what the United States is. But it is also part of what the United States is – without that flag, the reality of that country would be different. It is not merely part of our concept of the United States but a key part of its reality.

Notice that a symbol may have a life of its own, but also die. The Confederate States ceased to exist as a separate entity in 1865, but their flag, the Stars-and-Bars, retains its resonance in American life. It is a symbol of something especially Southern, revered and flown by many as a symbol (and not merely a sign) of identity. Another symbol might lose all such force. Whether the flag of Bessarabia has symbolic significance for anyone, I cannot tell – for me it would just be a sign of a long-gone geographical unit.

According to Tillich, religious language has the characteristics of symbol. If I say, 'God is Love', then that utterance is not merely a sign of what God is, but is a participation in the reality of God. Tillich adds that the term is both 'affirmed and negated' by the reality of God. It is affirmed because God really is love, but negated because the human term is so utterly inadequate as a description of God.

The obvious question is whether we are any further forward than with analogy. A positive feature of Tillich's approach is that by stressing the symbolic nature of religious language, Tillich reminds us starkly of the ever-present danger of anthropo-morphizing God.

On the other hand, questions have been raised, rightly, not least by John Hick,[5] about the notion that a symbol 'participates in that to which it points'. What precisely is the symbol in the sentence 'God is good'. Is the symbol the entire proposition? Or is it the underlying concept of 'the goodness of God'. Tillich does not explain precisely what he means by 'participation': and my words about God do not par-ticipate in his nature in the way that a flag is part of the life of a nation. And there is a particular danger in symbol. The Stars-and-Bars represents no current political reality. What that flag represents is an idea (perhaps an ideal) in the heads and hearts of those for whom it has meaning. If that is true, does it represent any reality beyond the creation of the beholders' minds? Symbols are made things, and we may represent and symbolize Utopia – or a God who existed no-where but in human minds.

J. H. Randall Jr. and Symbols as Non-Cognitive

Tillich's use of symbols is cognitive – it is perfectly possible to ask whether they are true or false. A non-cognitive analysis has been offered by John Hermann Randall Jr. (1899–1980)[6], based on Tillich. He argues that religious symbols are both non-cognitive and non-representative.

Randall argues that religion is a human activity which makes a contribution to man's culture. It speaks in a special way.

Think about music. A great piece of music speaks to us in a way that cannot be translated into anything else. Music cannot adequately be represented by a painting or by a description (one of the most toe-curling moments in literature is E. M. Forster's attempt to put Beethoven's Fifth Symphony into words). Music also touches parts of our being that nothing else can – it awakens in us emotions like no other. As Randall says of symbols:

> They make us receptive to qualities of the world encountered; and they open our hearts to the new qualities with which that world, in cooperation with the spirit of man, can clothe itself. They enable us to see and feel the religious dimension of our world better, the 'order of splendor', and of man's experience in and with it. They teach us how to find the Divine; they show us visions of God. Ibid., p. 129.

We should notice that this is nothing to do with a God who is another Being; for Randall God is our ideals, an intellectual symbol for what we feel as the Divine, for the religious dimension of our spirituality. A religious believer would object that this is not what she means by God, and would ask the difference between this 'Divine' and a figment of our imagination and emotions. For Randall, religion is a human enterprise which performs a valuable cultural function. The believer would claim that the God in whom she believes is not reducible to an art form.

Myth

Perhaps, of course, God really is just a myth. But a deeper sense of myth suggests that mythology is a way of understanding deeper reality. A Greek myth is a story, to be sure, but it is more than that as it resonates through our culture: stories of Odysseus and Theseus are tales also of human searches for certainty and for hearth and home in a strange world we scarcely understand.

We need to move beyond thinking of myth as simply untrue and to consider the ways in which myths could be a mode of understanding. Plato argued that myths, although fictitious, should be as close to truth as possible.[7] Often a myth is used to fill a gap in historical understanding where there is a lack of materials. For example, the writers of scripture lacked historical facts either about the beginning of the world or the genesis of mankind, but, certain there was a beginning, created myths to express it. Most scholars would accept Genesis as mythological, which is not quite the same as saying it is untrue. Remember what was said about cognitive and non-cognitive language. To ask whether a novel is true or false is simply to ask the wrong type of question.

In exactly the same way, it may be inappropriate to ask whether Genesis – or any other myth – is *true*. Rather, we perhaps need to ask whether it contains truth, and, if so, what that truth might be. A novel is not true, but we might describe it as 'true to life' or as containing 'truth' about human relationships. Great art gives us truths than can be expressed in no literal scientific way. Someone's love for another may be described in scientific terms as such and such a chemical reaction, the working of this or that brain activity or gland – but the bald scientific facts do not describe the inner reality of what it is truly to love this person. A poem, with all its conceits, may come closer to the lived reality of the meaning of this person's love for another. And it is not a lie.

If these thoughts are correct, then the truth within a myth might be more fully expressed than by a cold account of historical fact. It may be that such an account takes us closer to the nature of religious belief in what it means to the believer from the perspective of faith.

G. K. Chesterton (1874–1936), writing of St Francis of Assisi, said:

> . . . to this great mystic his religion was not a thing like a theory but a thing like a love-affair. G. K. Chesterton: *St Francis of Assisi*, Sheed and Ward, p. 16.

If poetry is the way to express understanding of a love affair, to convey something of the truth of what that might mean *to the lover*, then perhaps myth in religion is best seen as an expression of the truth of faith to the believer, written from the perspective of faith.

Taking such a view nevertheless runs counter to an important trend in twentieth-century biblical studies. Rudolf Bultmann (1884–1976), one of the greatest New Testament scholars, argued that modern understanding requires the reader to demythologize scripture. To read the Gospels is to return to a pre-scientific world picture, with heaven just 'up there' behind the clouds and hell just 'down below' – a three-storied universe. Science has shown the error of such a primitive view. We need to understand the universe in a much more sophisticated way. We think that the three synoptic Gospels – Matthew, Mark and Luke – were based on a collection of sayings of Jesus – which is known as *Quelle* (German for 'spring' or 'source'), commonly known as Q. Around these sayings and the indisputable fact of Jesus' crucifixion, the writers constructed their stories. Bultmann argues that the greatness of Jesus is emphasized by the construction of miracle stories – myths to express his power. Additionally, to bring out the significance of a given saying of Jesus, it would be woven into a little moral story, called an *apothegm*. These stories obviously are not literally true. For example, Jesus is portrayed as eating with publicans and sinners, and the Pharisees enter the house to question him. As Bultmann notes, no Pharisee would be seen dead in such a place. What matters is the significance of the story. For Bultmann, our need is to demythologize scripture, to return to the *kerygma*, the underlying message of Christ.

Bultmann's views are controversial, not least because of his interpretation of the content of the *kerygma*. But perhaps Bultmann's approach is mistaken. Rather than stripping out the myths from Scripture, perhaps the task of the believer might not be to deny that the myths are myth, but rather to accept that they are myths and to try to discern what truths they might contain.

STRETCH AND CHALLENGE

Incarnational Meaning

An interesting theory of meaning is offered by John Hick. This is the notion of Incarnational Meaning. This notion makes sense for Christianity but not for other faiths. The idea is simple. Christians believe that Jesus is the Son of God, the Second Person of the Trinity – God incarnate. This means that Christians are presented with God in human terms – we can, for example, see what God's love means in human life, because we are able to see its human aspect in Jesus' life and actions.

The problem with this initially attractive thesis is that it does not work for all claimed characteristics of God. If Jesus had the limitations of all mankind, we cannot see in Jesus what it means to be omnipotent or omniscient. Christianity insists on the radical humanity of Jesus as much as on his Godhead. This means that Jesus took on the fullness of human features – as Jesus in Palestine, he was not omniscient or omnipotent – he had to learn of his mission and to struggle with human emotions, as in Gethsemane. If he were not limited in this way, the Incarnation would become a sham, his body a mere shell in which a non-human mind lurked.

Further, we know comparatively little about Jesus. The Gospels are brief accounts of a life and ministry, Jesus' appearance is not described, there are differing accounts of events in different Gospels, and many of Jesus' reported sayings are ambiguous. There is the possibility that the believer invents Jesus in his own way, just as for many the image of Jesus is that of the bearded, flowing-locked creation of Western art. The real Jesus is elusive, and thus it is difficult to read off from his life what words and descriptions mean in relation to God.

A Non-Cognitive Analysis

An interesting non-cognitive analysis of religious language was offered by R. B. Braithwaite in his *An Empiricist's View of Religious Belief*, published in 1955.[8] Braithwaite (1900–90) was an important figure. He was the fourth member of the Cambridge Philosophy Department with Wittgenstein, G. E. Moore and Russell. Following a profound conversion experience he became a devout Anglican, having been brought up as a Quaker.

His theory was that religious language is fundamentally ethical language. When someone says, 'God is love', he is making a declaration that he intends to act in an agapeistic way, when he says, 'God is Truth', he declares his intention to act in a truthful way. So, the key is that these sentences are statements of *intention*.

But, there is a flaw in this approach. For Braithwaite, to say 'God is Truth' means 'I intend to act to act truthfully' or, 'I intend not to lie'. But this is absurd. It is perfectly logically possible to say 'God is Truth but *I* intend to lie'. That sentence makes sense – after all, I am not God (even in my deluded moments), and the descriptions that apply to me are different from those that apply to God. God may, to my belief, be pure truth, but I might be a dreadful liar. If Braithwaite is right, my position would be:

God is Truth but I intend to lie ≡ I intend not to lie but I intend to lie

The first of the two sentences makes perfect sense, in that there is no logical inconsistency, but the second is a contradiction, so 'God is Truth' cannot mean the same as 'I intend not to lie.' My descriptions of God do not necessarily express my intentions.

A second feature of Braithwaite's approach is to argue that what makes a Christian belief different from a Moslem one is not the ethical intent but the associated stories. For instance, the Christian may feel motivated by Jesus' heroic virtue or by parables such as that of the Good Samaritan. To associate her own intention with these stories helps to bolster her resolve. The Buddhist or the Hindu might be supported by different stories. What makes religious faiths different is the different associated stories. Braithwaite argues that it is irrelevant whether these stories are actually true. The effect of the parables is quite separate from whether Jesus recounts actual events. Braithwaite makes much of the spiritual effect of Bunyan's *Pilgrim's Progress*, which profoundly shaped British religious faith and practice, yet which was known by all its readers to be fiction.

The obvious problem with these arguments is that it matters to believers that what they believe is *true*. They do not take the Nicene Creed or other statement of faith as a list of ethical intentions and a few stories whose truth is irrelevant. Nor is it clear that *every* religious sentence is either a statement of ethical intent or a story. To say 'God is Immutable' surely cannot mean 'I intend to be Immutable', as immutability is not possible to me; and it is not much of a story, either. Braithwaite's account seems too far removed from the actual life and belief of religious people to be credible.

Exercise and Examination Advice

Make a list of the following terms in your notes and make sure you research them until you have a clear understanding of what each means:

Apophatic way

Via negativa

Cataphatic

Via positiva

Doctrine of Analogy

Univocal

Equivocal

Analogical

Attribution

Proportion

Sign

Symbol

Anthropomorphizing

Non-cognitive

Myth

You should also be able to demonstrate a good understanding of the views of writers such as:

Pseudo-Dionysius

St Thomas Aquinas

Moses Maimonides

John McQuarrie

Ian Ramsey

Karl Barth

Paul Tillich

J. H. Randall

Rudolf Bultmann

R. B. Braithwaite

This has been a long chapter and has dealt with a significant range of concepts through an equally significant range of philosophical writers. This is definitely a topic where a class could more effectively work in teams; possibly preparing PowerPoint presentations on the different areas and then sharing them with the whole class. For example, one group could explore the work of Pseudo-Dionysius and Moses Maimonides, not only preparing the presentation but also putting together some useful notes on the topic of the 'via negativa' or 'apophatic way' which would include quotations from the relevant writers. At the same time, another group could do the same for the writings of St Thomas Aquinas, putting together notes on what is meant by analogy and exploring the usefulness or otherwise of equivocal and univocal language. Some may feel that the teachers should do this for them; however I can guarantee that you will remember research you have to do for yourself much better than anything which is just handed to you.

Once again, I would like to emphasis the importance of checking primary sources as often as you can while you do this exercise; textbooks have a habit of passing on errors in a 'chinese whisper' kind of way.

Having done that, you could try the following question:

To what extent do myths give a better insight to the nature of God than symbols?

Notes

1. Friedrich von Hügel (1921) *Essays and Addresses on the Philosophy of Religion* (First Series, J. M Dent and Sons), pp. 102–3.
2. John McQuarrie (1967) *God-Talk* (SCM), p. 214.
3. Ian T. Ramsey (1957) *Religious Language* (SCM).
4. T. T. Clark, 1957.
5. The following paragraph is indebted to John Hick's discussion in his *Philosophy of Religion*.
6. J. H. Randall, Jr. (1958) *The Role of Knowledge in Western Religion* (Beacon Press), especially pp. 128–9.
7. Plato, *Republic*, ii, 382d.
8. Cambridge University Press.

Religious Language – Language Games 5

Introduction

Much interesting philosophical work in Philosophy of Religion in the past 50 years or so has been done in the name of extending the ideas of the later Wittgenstein. Wittgenstein himself wrote little directly about religion, although he did discuss it in tutorials, but various followers and disciples, including Elizabeth Anscombe, Peter Winch, Rush Rhees and D. Z. Phillips have extended his ideas into their work.

A central problem with Wittgenstein's work is that his statements were frequently very obscure and much that we have from him consists of edited versions of scattered notes and notebooks, published after his death by various pupils and followers. And philosophers have to contend with two Wittgensteins, the early and the late: it is important not to confuse the earlier with the later. It is in the later Wittgenstein, perhaps especially in *The Blue and Brown Books* as well as *Philosophical Investigations*, that we find the bones of Language Game theory.

A biographical note might be useful. Ludwig Wittgenstein was born in 1889 to a wealthy and highly talented Viennese family (His brother, Paul, was a concert pianist who in the First World War lost his right arm and used family wealth to commission piano concertos for the left hand from composers such as Prokofiev and Ravel). He studied engineering, first in Berlin, then in Manchester, but felt increasingly drawn to philosophy. In 1912, he moved to Cambridge, where he worked closely with Bertrand Russell. On the outbreak of war, in 1914, he went home to Austria to join the army, fighting on the Italian front, where he was captured and became a prisoner of war. During this period, he wrote his *Tractatus Logico-Philosophicus*. This was the only book of his published in his lifetime.

In the *Tractatus*, Wittgenstein argued that many of the traditional problems of philosophy were actually problems of language. If only we were to construct an appropriate logical language on the lines he set out, it would be possible not to *solve* traditional problems, but to *dissolve* them. They would not be problems, but shown to be linguistic errors. He accompanied this notion with his *picture theory* of language, arguing that language is a kind of pictorial representation of the world, though we often rearrange the pictorial elements in ways which do not directly represent the reality of the world. He completed the short but immensely difficult book with the words 'whereof we cannot speak, thereof we should be silent.' This was taken by the Logical Positivists as a declaration that such things as religious propositions were meaningless. That is probably not what Wittgenstein meant – as we shall see.

Wittgenstein returned briefly to Cambridge, but believed he ought not to draw his salary – having resolved all the problems of philosophy, there was nothing left to say. He returned to Austria, and worked as a schoolteacher in the Tirol from 1920 until 1926. His disciplinary methods were considered too robust, and he resigned after knocking a pupil senseless. He then worked as an architect in Vienna, building a mansion for his sister (today it is an embassy). During these years he met and discussed ideas with members of the Vienna Circle. His discussions included religion. He is recorded as saying:

> Is speech essential for religion? I can quite well imagine a religion in which there are no doctrines and hence nothing is said. Obviously the essence of religion can have nothing to do with the fact that speech occurs – or rather: if speech does occur this is a component of religious behaviour and not a theory. Therefore nothing turns on whether the words are true, false, or nonsensical.[1]

This suggests that his silence does not indicate that religious sentences are meaningless, as well as revealing something of his fundamental disagreements with the Vienna Circle.

By this time, he was moving away from the views of the *Tractatus*. No longer did he believe that we could construct one master logical language. He repudiated the picture theory of meaning and developed the work we know as the later Wittgenstein. In 1929 he returned to Cambridge, becoming Professor of Philosophy: he remained there for the remainder of his teaching life, dying in 1951. His work became known principally through word from his pupils and his rather odd personal life (he lived without furniture, Bertrand Russell having sold his stored furniture to send him the money to leave the prisoner-of-war camp and return to Britain) and strong character gave him guru status. The publication of his *Philosophical Investigations*, posthumously, in 1953, was a major event in disseminating his ideas.

Language Games

Consider your own life. We live our lives in sections – perhaps three, four or more of these. We may, for instance, have part of our lives as members of families, in another chunk we are students of Philosophy, in another with friends, in another perhaps as a member of church, synagogue or mosque, in another as customers of a bank, in another at a part-time job. We recognize that each of these aspects of life has a certain way of speaking. In our families, we often have turns of phrase that would make little sense to those outside the family group. The language we use with our friends is not identical with that we use in more formal situations – such as in the classroom or when giving evidence in court. When we learn a new subject, what we are doing is to learn a new language. When a computer novice hears computer buffs in conversation, he does not begin to understand their language. Once he understands, then he can join the conversation.

It is this type of notion which underlies language game theory. When I learn the language of a subject, or those of the special world of my family, I am learning the rules of a game – the language game. For Wittgenstein, I am a player of games. Each game has its own rules, and one does not play one game by the rules of another. The rules of rugby and those of cricket are different. To speak of a ball in one is to speak of a cork, leather and twine spherical object which is small and hard with sewn seams. A rugby ball is something very different. And a bat is very different in talk of the animal kingdom from what it is in cricket. A 'slip' is something different in an office, in cricket, in fashion, in a theatre, in descriptions of my attempts at ice-skating, and so on.

For the later Wittgenstein, we cannot ask the absolute meaning of any word – only its meaning *in use*, that is, its meaning in a particular game. To ask what I mean by a 'slip' is to ask about the game in which I am using it. And that meaning is determined by the rules of the particular game.

It is important to notice that for Wittgenstein *there are only the games*. We cannot get 'outside' the games to ask the 'real' meaning of words. We can only play another game. To ask the real meaning – perhaps the dictionary meaning – of a word is not to step outside the world of games, but rather to play the lexicography game.

This has several significant consequences. Most obviously we cannot get outside games – our linguistic life is a matter of our competence in playing different games: I may confidently play a greater or smaller number of games than you; and they will almost certainly not be precisely the same sets of games. We need further to note that we cannot say that one game is intrinsically better or more true than another. Its value and meaning are determined by its own rules.

Importantly, we should note that the language games do not *reflect* reality: they *make* it. That is, the world as we know it is the world expressed in our games. I cannot play a 'real-world' game that is superior to any other game I play: it remains still a game – another game among games. What the world means to me – what it *is* to me – is determined by the games I play. Wittgenstein has moved away from any notion that language involves pictures of reality, or that there is any one master form of language. If this is so, we cannot ask what reality is like – we can merely play another form of language game – the 'reality' language game.

We might note that on this analysis, traditional views of cognitive and non-cognitive language become difficult, but we can see that this theory is essentially *beyond* that discussion. There are games in which it makes perfect sense to say that it is false to say that Michael scored a century or that Hugh is sewing a strip of ribbon onto a dress. But in the game of writing poetry, given sentences may be non-cognitive – all depends on the rules as they affect particular usages of words. It is the rules of the game that determine whether sentences within it are to be understood cognitively or not. In the games of physics or geography they presumably are: in poetry or the language of fiction they are not.

The Religious Significance of Language Games

As noted, Wittgenstein himself wrote little directly about religion. Nevertheless, many of his followers, including Elizabeth Anscombe, Rush Rhees, and later, D. Z. Phillips, were devout believers. They argued that this analysis had a profound effect on the understanding of religious belief and faith.

An obvious area would be the question of the debate between theists and atheists. If Wittgenstein is right, the believer and the non-believer would be playing different language games. In the case of the believer, 'God exists' would be a sentence filled with meaning: God would be part of the reality created by the language game she played. But to the non-believer, playing the atheist game, the term 'God' would be an empty phrase, perhaps stripped of meaning.

The consequences of such an understanding are significant. If we say that God is a reality in the theist language game and a non-reality in the atheist game, we would appear to be guilty of the logical error of excluded middle, that is, attempting to say that God both really is and really is not, which looks absurd. But to ask this question is at odds with the theory of language games – our question is a 'real reality' type of question, which language game theory rules out. To ask it, we are just playing another game, and it is a game which cannot be thought of as somehow superior to another, whether atheist or theist.

Wittgenstein enthusiasts have developed these notions in different ways. For example, for Don Cupitt and his followers in the Sea of Faith movement, it has meant denying God as a reality in himself. For Cupitt, God is not something that exists, but simply a reality within the community of faith. Cupitt argues that Christianity involves a special form of life, with special values and meanings. He recommends his own non-metaphysical approach as the best way to live.[2]

D. Z. Phillips, perhaps the most significant Wittgensteinian working in the Philosophy of Religion, argued differently. (Phillips himself developed his work from that of Rush Rhees, with whom he worked closely. It was said of Phillips that for him, Wittgenstein was God, and Rush Rhees his pope. When Rhees died, Phillips bought for himself the plot at Rhees' feet in Swansea cemetery.) He picked up the notion from Wittgenstein of 'forms of life'.

Wittgenstein's own references to forms of life are scattered through his work. Patrick Sherry argues that the concept of forms of life is developed by the followers of Wittgenstein rather than by Wittgenstein himself.[3] Sherry suggests that in some ways, Phillips misunderstands Wittgenstein. Nevertheless, we can understand Phillips' view. He quotes with approval a comment by Wittgenstein in *Philosophical Investigations*: 'Philosophy may in no way interfere with the actual use of language; it can in the end only describe it. For it cannot give it any foundation either. It leaves everything as it is.'[4] For Phillips, the philosopher's task was not to comment on the truth of religious statements, but to question and clarify their meaning. As he says, the task of philosophy is not 'to settle the question of whether a man is talking to God or not, but to ask what it means to affirm or deny that a man is talking to God.'[5] Unlike Cupitt, Phillips does not deny the objective existence of God. He simply denies that it is part of the philosopher's task to determine (he cannot) God's existence. Phillips argued that to ask whether God exists is a question in the religious form of life, rather than a scientific one. It is question beyond the philosopher's remit:

We resist mystery because we tend to give the primary place to explanation. But religion brings to our attention the limits of human existence, limits for which no further explanations can be found. Religion, *in this context*, asks us to die to the understanding. . . . In religion, meeting what confronts us is a form of acceptance in terms of the grace of God. D. Z. Phillips: *From Fantasy to Faith*, SCM, 2006, p. 228.

This position is very different from Cupitt's. Phillips argues that *as philosophers* we can only look, coolly, at the meanings and grammar of sentences in religious sentences. For him there is a reality beyond the game with which we are confronted, whereas for Cupitt the only reality of God is found *within* the language game. Cupitt endorses a non-realist approach to religious truth: Phillips rejects it.

Objections to Language Games

The very notion of language games has been the subject of much heated debate in the past 50 years. A major critic was Ernest Gellner, whose *Words and Things* (Routledge) is a blistering and often very funny attack on Wittgensteinian assumptions, with a preface by Bertrand Russell who likens the obsession with meaning to those who are continually sharpening their tools but never using them. He compares the obsession with the meaning of words with someone who takes apart a perfectly performing clock and then wonders why it no longer works.

   Probably the most significant criticism of language games is that they are circular. Whence comes the meaning of a word? From the language game from which it takes its meaning. But whence does the language game get its meaning? From the words that constitute it. It seems that for a given language game to make sense there needs to be some external link to give meaning to the whole. The question is whether language games can have the autonomy which Phillips – and others – attribute to them.

   For Phillips, science and religion are different types of discourse, and we can *justify* neither. The game is basic. (There seems to be something foundationalist here, though Phillips argues otherwise). If this is the case, then science and theology could say nothing to each other: yet the very question of science and religion is a significant point of discussion within both communites.[6] Patrick Sherry argues that:

> . . . whilst it may be silly to ask for a *general* justification of religion or science, we can certainly discuss *particular* ones, e.g Christianity or astrology (incidentally, although the question 'Is science true?' is absurd, the question 'Why pursue science?' is not.) Patrick Sherry: *Religion, Truth and Language-Games*, Macmillan, 1977, p. 30.

Sherry's point is that language theorists rule out many different types of question as being based on failure to understand the rules of the game. But these are real questions within the game. To develop Sherry's point, in the community of faith, God is not simply a given term, with meaning to the community. It is central to the very notion of faith that God might not exist – his non-existence is a real possibility which the true believer accepts. That is why she has faith rather than certainty. If the real possibility of the non-reality of God is part of the believer's religious language game, then it is a game that the non-believer himself can play. The games of God's existence or non-existence are not separable.

There may be another circularity in the theory of games. If there are only games, each with equal legitimacy, how then are we to treat the entire theory of language games? Is this just the 'Language Game language game,' no more significant or important than any other? Why should this be privileged over any other? The truth of language game theory would seem to lie in itself, an assertion underlying the entire theory, but beyond justification. There is nothing outside the language game – on the theory nothing could be outside – to legitimate its claims.

J. L. Austin and Locutions

Among those influenced by Wittgenstein was the brilliant young philosopher J. L. Austin (1911–60). In a famous paper, 'Other Minds', from 1946,[7] he developed the idea of 'performatory utterances'. In this, he was considering not simply what sentences *mean*, but what they *do*. For example, to say *'I promise'* does not merely describe the fact that I am making a promise: it is the very *act* of making the promise. To say 'I am warning you' to someone is an action as well as a speech act.

This type of thought led him to develop the notion of the *illocutionary* use of language. Suppose a lecturer who is writing a paper is at home keeping an eye on young children. He is trying to work, but they keep running in and out of his study. He tells them to go downstairs and play quietly. They run out of the room, leaving the door open. He calls after them: 'The door is open.' The words, just on the page, look like a statement of fact, but the sentence is doing something else. He is saying, 'The door is open. It should not be. Come back and shut it.' In making this utterance, 'The door is open', the lecturer is also performing an act: the act of expressing disapproval and giving an order. The meaning of the sentence, which is an act, lies in what it does.

But a different usage – what Austin calls a *locution* – happens in *perlocutionary* use of language. In this case, the sentence *is* the act, and not simply the performance of the act. An obvious case is, 'I promise . . .' It is the saying 'I promise' which *is* the act of promising.

These views of Austin have profound resonance for considering the religious meaning of words. Perlocutionary uses would include, 'I baptise thee', 'I ordain' and so on. And prayer involves illocutionary use – what act is the saying of a prayer, such as the rosary, perform.

This approach by Austin may prove to be one of the richest means of understanding the many uses of religious language. Above all, it serves the valuable function of reminding us – against those keen to reduce religious language to science or verifiable sentences or some other single formula – that not only is it something that contains a wide variety of possible levels of meaning, but also a multitude of uses and actions.

STRETCH AND CHALLENGE

Wittgensteinian Fideism

An interesting question was raised by A. J. Ayer in his inaugural lecture at Oxford.[8] If each language game has its own reality, are not Phillips and others committed to accepting as legitimate talk about fairies and witches? Just because someone describes another as 'bewitched' it does not follow that there actually are demons in the world, and there are good reasons why one might want to characterize that entire language game us untrue, and not simply to say that a given sentence is true or false only within the game.

Considerations such as these led to a long-running argument, principally between Phillips and Kai Nielsen, with others joining in.[9] Following the publication of Phillips' *The Concept of Prayer*, in 1965, Nielsen wrote an essay in *Philosophy* called 'Wittgensteinian Fideism'. The debate between the two ceased only on Phillips' sudden death in 2006. The original article was largely an attack on Peter Winch, but it was Phillips who devoted most time to defending the cause of Wittgenstein.

Nielsen's charge was that forms of life are not amenable to criticism – each is what it is on its own terms. Each form has its own rules of reality, intelligibility and reason. As a result, notions of reality, intelligibility and reason become ambiguous as their precise meaning can only be determined *within the given discourse*. There is therefore no position (Nielsen calls it an 'Archimedean point'[10]) from which a philosopher or anyone else can criticize a given discourse. If this is the case, then to be within the game of faith, means that faith becomes simply fideism.

Fideism is generally considered heretical view: it is simply the assertion of faith without any reason for it except the assertion. This approach to faith has been specifically condemned by the Roman Catholic faith as it is a denial of God-given reason. To believe for no more reason than that one says it is true gives no more strength to faith than a parent who asserts something is the case, 'because I say so!' Fideism is a denial of reason. If there is no reason outside the game or form of life for the belief, for joining the game, then it seems just a matter of assertion. Remarks by Philips, such as those quoted above about religion being beyond understanding or explanation, appear to give evidence to strengthen Nielsen's case.

The essence of Phillip's detailed response is that the work of the Wittgensteinian analyst is not simply one of blind faith. Much religious belief is confused and muddled. The labour of determining true meaning requires intellectual rigour and is arduous – it is neither blind nor simple. It is in that way that justice can actually be done to competing views on religious belief. Phillips' last words on the subject were:

> Philosophical contemplation seeks to do justice to belief and atheism, to the confusions and the sense that can be found in each. An atheism that holds that *all* religious beliefs are either false or incoherent will be unable to do that. But, then, it has always been recognised that one's own beliefs can get in the way of the kind of attention called for by a contemplative conception of philosophy. Kai Nielsen and D. Z. Phillips, *Wittgensteinian Fideism*, SCM, 2005, p. 371.

Whether that really answers the claim that Neilsen makes is open to question. It is one thing to argue that the language game approach does justice to atheism and belief in that it resolves conceptual muddles *within* those claims; but it cannot settle, as Phillips acknowledges, the *external* question of whether the forms of life themselves are true. Of course, it may be that the Wittgensteinian claim that there are only the forms and nothing outside that can justify them, is correct; but there seems no possible way to establish that, as the possibility of an external justification is ruled out.

Exercise and Examination Advice

Make a list of the following terms in your notes and make sure you research them until you have a clear understanding of what each means:

Picture theory of language

Early Wittgenstein

Later Wittgenstein

Language Games

You should also be able to demonstrate a good understanding of the views of writers such as:

Wittgenstein

Elizabeth Anscombe

Rush Rhees

D. Z. Phillips

Bertrand Russell

A possible way of approaching this topic would be to get yourselves into sets of 'interest groups' within the class, such as rugby players, hockey players, writers of computer programmes, footballers, fans of TV programmes or groups who know each other from outside the school or college. In smaller classes, this could be done in as individuals. Then make lists of the words that you use which are particular to your group, especially words which have other meanings in more ordinary contexts. Then you could share them with other sets exploring whether or not they can understand your use of the word without your explaining the context.

Alternatively, you could look at how comedians and comic writers use the ideas of words out of context to make humorous comments. One of my favourites, for example, is *The Hitch Hiker's Guide to the Galaxy* where Douglas Adams made use of lateral thinking to make his readers laugh and at times think; the idea was to give the impression that one thing was meant when the word was being used in a completely different context. So, for example, when Arthur Dent cannot see why travelling in hyperspace is a problem as it has been described as being '. . . unpleasantly like being drunk'. His friend, Ford Prefect, replies 'Have you ever asked a glass of water?'

I am sure that the class can between you come up with a good number of examples of this kind of thing which should provoke a discussion of the extent to which much of our language would seem to be arbitrarily given meaning by the context in which it is used, or the game we are playing at the time. You could then explore together the question of whether or not any group committed to a particular way of describing the world can ever talk seriously with another. A more serious way to explore this issue might be to explore how often a group of terrorists have become a Government, provoking the maxim, 'Today's terrorist is tomorrow's freedom fighter.'

Then you could try to answer the following question:

'The picture theory of language gives us a better way of understanding the world than language game theory.' Discuss.

Notes

1. Quoted in Patrick Sherry (1977) *Religion, Truth and Language-Games* (Macmillan), 1977, p. 1.
2. See his *Taking Leave of God*, SCM, 1980 and *The Sea of Faith*, BBC Publications, 1984 as admirably lucid expositions of his view.
3. Patrick Sherry (1977) *Religion, Truth and Language-Games* (Macmillan), p. 4.
4. Ludwig Wittgenstein (1963) *Philosophical Investigations* (OUP), p. 124.
5. D. Z. Phillips (1965) *The Concept of Prayer* (Routledge), p. 37.
6. For an interesting discussion of this with particular reference to language games, see: William H. Austin: *The Relevance of Natural Science to Theology*, Macmillan, 1976, especially Chapter 5.
7. J. L. Austin (1961) 'Other Minds', *Philosophical Papers*, Clarendon, Oxford, 1961, pp. 44–84, but see especially 63–74. The notion is further developed in J. L. Austin: *How to Do Things with Words*, Oxford, 1964.
8. A. J. Ayer (1963) *The Concept of a Person and Other Essays*, p. 18.
9. The ins and outs of the debate may be enjoyed in: Kai Nielsen and D. Z. Phillips, *Wittgensteinian Fideism*, SCM, 2005.
10. *Ibid.*, p. 22.

Religious Experience 6

Introduction

Many have claimed that their knowledge of God is a matter of direct experience. In some way they have encountered him. This is a tricky claim to deal with, because whatever it means to encounter God, it cannot be like meeting another human being. None knows what God looks like – there is nothing he would be like – and we have no identification even for his human form if we believe that Jesus is God. Of Jesus, we have no photographs but only the imaginings of later artists to give us our impressions of him. The ever-present danger of delusion is always with us. Bertrand Russell commented that some people drink too much and see snakes, while others fast too much and see God. Long before Russell, the great philosopher, Thomas Hobbes (1588–1679) remarked that when a man says that God spoke to him in a dream it '. . . is no more than to say he dreamed that God spoke to him.'[1] We are well aware of the mind-altering effects of drink or drugs as well as mental illness. And we know that all of us are capable of mistaken perception, as when we call to a friend in the street only to find a stranger turning to us. We make mistakes and misremember, misunderstand or see things not really there. We sometimes are tricked by the light, occasionally by deliberate fraud.

We are troubled also by the question of the privacy of experience. I can never experience things as you do – I do not even know whether when we both call something 'blue' or 'sweet' that the experience you have – the 'what it feels like to me' – is the same as mine. I cannot share your religious experience – I can only feel mine. Even when a group claims to have experienced God, for each person in the group, it remains an individual experience.

Sometimes people point to the sincerity of the witness who claims the religious experience. But that is not firm evidence – honest people are sometimes sincere in holding beliefs quite contrary to those held by other equally sincere and honest persons. You may be sincere, but sincerely wrong. Any policeman will tell many tales of wholly honest witnesses giving wildly different accounts of the same event. No one gives an unvarnished description of an event – the act of putting it into words is itself an act of interpretation, a translation with all the attendant difficulties. That act of translation is itself affected by the witness' prior experience, understanding, intelligence, vocabulary and so on.

But neither does it follow from these doubts that every account a witness gives will be untrue, nor that it does not have any basis in fact. I may get wrong in my teaching the details of this or that philosophical theory, but it does not follow from my misinterpretation that Aquinas or Kant did not say what they did. There remains a truth behind my misrepresentation.

Types of Religious Experience

There are several types of claimed religious experience. Some are corporate, when a group is affected, some individual. But it is important to remember that even when an experience is corporate, each member of the group will directly know only her own experience – other people might be faking their emotions and actions to belong to the group. But she herself will only directly experience what she feels. If I say someone is angry, or happy, or embarrassed, I am drawing an inference from her perceived behaviour – her scowls, laughter, tears and so on – but I am not feeling those emotions as she does. That I might feel such-and-such at the sight of her reactions does not mean that I am feeling her feelings. That is true both when I attempt to judge your individual behaviour as well as that in a group.

Corporate experiences cause special problems, not least because we know that people behave in groups in ways that they would not as individuals, perhaps joining in the collective activity and emotion out of a feeling of wanting to belong. An individual can draw strength from a group to act in ways he might not when alone – a ruffian might alone do no harm to passers-by, but when in a group of similar toughs behave more boldly and more violently. Group hysteria is a recognized effect in social psychology. One might imagine that corporate religious experiences give better evidence of divine origin than individual ones. In fact, the opposite is probably the case: the opportunity for error and delusion is increased.

Probably the most famous modern example of corporate experience is the odd phenomenon known as the *Toronto Blessing*. A rather odd set of events began on 10 January 1984 at the Toronto Airport Vineyard Christian Fellowship. This was a very evangelical organization already interested in charismatic worship. Randy Clark, a pastor from St Louis, Missouri, had been invited to the church, to minister. He had been much influenced by Rodney Howard-Browne, a South African evangelical preacher who ministered, in Louisville, Kentucky. The latter had become involved in the phenomenon of 'Holy Laughter' which was said to be sign of the Holy Spirit, and other manifestations. In Randy Clark's service, after preaching and hymns, the Toronto congregation manifested what they saw as signs of God – uncontrollable laughter, speaking in incomprehensible language, rolling on the floor and various other activities. This was taken by many to be a certain sign of God's action. Many tens of thousands have subsequently visited Toronto to witness to what they believe to be this manifestation of the Spirit and Vineyard Churches have begun elsewhere in the world.

Others have been more sceptical, arguing that people were already inclined to behave in such a way because they had already chosen an evangelical and charismatic form of faith. Some critics pointed to the way in which at atmosphere had already buit-up within the congregation through prayers, hymns and preaching about the work of the spirit. Some evangelical believers argued that such manifestations might simply be the work of malicious demons holding up believers to ridicule. Questions arose about people speaking in tongues. In the *Acts of the Apostles*, the apostles, after their Pentecost experience, go out to the assembled crowds and speak to them in such a way that every member of the crowd, regardless of his own language, can hear and understand the message. The one thing the gift of tongues was not was to be incomprehensible. Other critics dismissed the event as straightforward hysteria and self-delusion. Theologically, one might ask what such an event might reveal of God? Does it show a God of Love, or simply God as a kind of master hypnotist – a magician? If a believer is so taken over, does God take away that believer's autonomy to believe or not? If God takes away the believer's reason, even for a while, does that believer become less than the human God made her to be? If human freedom is so important to true faith, a simple being taken over by a force looks rather too much like coercion. And why would God expend so much effort to do things of this kind for a relatively small group in Toronto while doing nothing for the starving of Somalia or the per- secuted believers (if belief is so crucial) in China and elsewhere? Some Christian critics of Toronto have argued that the God allegedly shown would be a God not worthy of belief.

A key problem for the theologian is that events such as the Toronto Blessing can obscure the variety of possible experience. Some claimed experience is very dramatic, such as recounted in *Acts*, when Saul is thrown from his horse on the way to Damascus, is blinded, hears a voice ('Saul, Saul, why do you persecute me?'), and is taken helpless to the city. There he undergoes a transformation, and becomes the great apostle to the Gentiles and eventual martyr for his faith. That is a *conversion experience* – as well as one of *visions* and *voices*. Nevertheless, as presented in Acts, Paul (as he becomes) is not simply taken over. What confronts him is as stark and dramatic as anything could be, but it is he who has to assent. His freedom not to assent is not taken away, and it takes him time to accept his new self. The sign that he has converted is his actions – his new way of life.

But the conversion of Saul is not a typical conversion experience. For many a process of conversion, whether from one faith to another, or from no faith at all, or, indeed, someone discovering a vocation to be a priest, is a gradual matter, with perhaps no Damascus moment so much as finding new ways of seeing the world. It might be just seeing ordinary people in new ways, meeting a particular person and being drawn by that person's character, or feeling in a personal way the call of the poor of Peru as a call from God. For many people, religious experience is a not a matter of loud noises, voices, high drama, of visions of eternity, but rather of experiencing ordinary things in a particular kind of way – perhaps in prayer, in joint activity with others, in aesthetic experience or just in the particularity and preciousness discerned in another. Mark Wynn[2] has pointed to the ways that particular places or pilgrimage can mediate the presence of God. When we see the world, our understanding is coloured by association. When I meet a friend, that meeting is coloured by associations – the things we have shared that affect the way we see each other, feel about each other. We are not neutral observers of the world, and our feelings towards each other do not simply come from nowhere. Think, for example, of how our perception of someone can be shaped when that person reminds us of someone else we once knew.

Religious Experience as 'Experiencing-As'

These thoughts might lead us to think of religious experience as simply a particular way of experiencing the world. John Hick has developed this idea from Wittgenstein's notion of 'seeing as'.

Wittgenstein, in *Philosophical Investigations*,[3] considered the philosophical significance of puzzle pictures. The one he considers is the duck-rabbit, which can be seen as both a duck and a rabbit. Other examples might be the picture that looks both like a young girl and an old crone, or the candlestick which can also be seen as two faces in profile. Wittgenstein's idea is that these are philosophically as well as psychologically interesting. Not least, they suggest that the world is never 'just' such and such: there is a variety of possible ways of seeing it.

Hick has interpreted this notion into a way[4] which moves from simply a matter of observation to a more holistic matter of total experience. This is an interesting notion, because it suggests that the religious believer is not perceiving anything different from the non-believer when she looks at the world, but instead perceives it in a different way. This can be related to John Wisdom's parable of the gardener, in which the two explorers in the garden come across exactly the same things in the garden, yet one sees the neatness as the work of an invisible gardener, while the other focuses on the patches of chaos, claiming that no gardener comes. Neither sees anything, or denies the evidence that the other points to, that the other does not.

This appears a promising way to interpret religious experience. The differences lie not so much in perceiving different things, but in perceiving the same things differently. But this view of things, reflecting a difference of attitude, sometimes called *Gestalt* experiences, may be insufficient as an understanding. Vincent Brümmer points out[5] that the original duck-rabbit is neither duck nor rabbit, but lines on a page, whereas the religious claim is to interpret the world as it really is. The believer is not merely having a different sort of experience but claiming that their perception is the *true* one. This claim is based on certain criteria drawn from the conceptual framework of their faith. Interpreting the experience is based on those criteria – the believer does not just *happen* to see something in religious terms in the way she might happen to see a given picture first as a duck and only subsequently as a rabbit. Religious believers believe that when they interpret their experiences of the world religiously, they are recognizing a true state of affairs, and not simply happening to take one particular view.

William James and the Character of Religious Experiences

The classic statement of religious experiences is found in William James' *The Varieties of Religious Experience*. William James (1842–1910), the elder brother of the novelist Henry James, was a pioneer in both psychology and philosophy, and one of the most distinguished of the Pragmatic school in American philosophy. He was deeply interested in the phenomenon of personal religion – rather less so, perhaps, in its institutional variety. The lectures which make up *The Varieties of Religious Experience* were originally given as the Gifford lectures in Edinburgh in 1901–02. They remain a masterpiece of religious thought.

His interest in human psychology is evident throughout. He attempts to define the nature of religious belief, and discusses at length different types of religious experience including a detailed study of conversion. In his lectures (XVI and XVII) on Mysticism, he identifies four characteristics of genuine mystical experience:

- *Ineffability*, that is, their being beyond the capacity of words to describe. He describes the mystical state of mind is 'negative' in that it knows that no words can begin to describe the nature of that experience.
- *Noetic quality*, which is that the experience is like a state of knowledge, but it is a type of knowledge beyond any normal experience. James says: 'They [religious experiences] are states of insight into depths of truth unplumbed by the discursive intellect. They are illuminations, revelations, full of significance and importance, all inarticulate though they remain; and as a rule they carry with them a curious sense of authority for aftertime.'
- *Transciency* – The experiences in themselves last only the briefest time, rarely more than half an hour or so, but their effects are life-changing.
- *Passivity* – People affected feel as if their own will is in abeyance as if in the grip of a superior power.

It would be wrong to assume from this that James believes that religious experiences are therefore true. They could be indicative of God. He does not discount – and indeed, discusses, the possibility that they might be the result of delusion, drunkenness or some other error. In his essay, 'The Will to Believe' (1897), he had already argued that one cannot fix a belief or draw a conclusion unless all other possibilities had been explored.

In *The Varieties of Religious Belief*, James points out that the interpretation of religious experiences is affected by what he describes as 'over-beliefs', by which he means the conceptual frameworks we have:

> Here the prophets of all the different religions come with their visions, voices, rapture, and other openings, supposed by each to authenticate his own peculiar faith. *Lecture XX.*

He argues that those among us not touched by these experiences will stand outside them, noting that they are used to validate a variety of different beliefs. For James, religious belief is a matter of an intellectual commitment – 'Among . . . sensibilities, intellectual ones play a decisive part.' Experiences may touch us, move us and teach us new facts which our intellects consider. For him, we do not simply interpret existing facts but may be given new ones:

> . . . Religion . . . is not a mere illumination of facts already . . . given, not a mere passion, like love, which views things in a rosier light. It is indeed that . . . But it is something more, namely, a postulator of new *facts* as well. The world interpreted religiously . . . must have . . . a *natural constitution* different at some point from that which a materialistic world would have. It must be such that different events can be expected in it, different conduct must be required. *Lecture XX.*

In constructing his argument, William James made much use of the work of St Teresa of Avila (1515–82). St Teresa underwent a series of visions at the age of 39 – she explained these in both her autobiography and in her *Interior Castle*. Some later commentators, as James noted, saw her visions as psychologically driven, perhaps the result of sexual frustration. St Teresa herself questioned whether they were the result of temptation of this kind, but decided they were not: she argued that if they were, she would have been left with sensations of disgust:

> . . . 'a genuine heavenly vision yields . . . a harvest of ineffable spiritual riches, and an admirable renewal of bodily strength. I alleged these reasons to those who so often accused my visions of being the work of the enemy of mankind and the sport of my imagination. . . . I showed them the jewels which the divine hand had left with me:- they were my actual dispositions . . . this improvement, palpable in all respects, far from being hidden, was brilliantly evident to all men. *Autobiography*, Ch. xxviii.

For St Teresa, the sign of the genuineness of a religious experience is the permanent change it creates in someone's character and whether it is consistent with the teachings of the Church in what it reveals. (A Christian sceptic might ask whether the Toronto Blessing meets these criteria.)

But this does not prove that the claimed experience reveals God: it demonstrates only the sincerity of the believer. If I sincerely believed I had received a vision of God, it would change my life, perhaps for the better: but my sincere belief might yet be mistaken.

STRETCH AND CHALLENGE

A. J. Ayer and Near-Death Experiences

In recent years, much has been made – in some quarters –of the phenomenon of near-death experiences and their evidential value. In 1975, Dr Raymond Moody published *Life After Life: The Investigation of a Phenomenon – Survival of Bodily Death*[6] which he has followed with further studies.[7] An enormous literature has grown up around this phenomenon.

It is often found among patients close to death, perhaps in hospital following a heart attack or some other severe trauma. Patients often report themselves to find their consciousness floating from their bodies, so that they might hover over their beds watching the crash team working on their bodies. There is also the experience of seeing a tunnel, normally with a brightly-lit world. This vision has various stages – not all who experience the phenomenon reach the fifth stage – most did not. The stages are:

1. feelings of peace and contentment,
2. a sense of detachment from the body,
3. 'the tunnel experience,' the sense of passing through darkness to light,

4. emerging into bright light, and

5. 'entering the light.'

For many, these experiences suggest the reality of both heaven and the God who provides it. Many report their beliefs strengthened and say that they look upon death with a new serenity.

But there is counter-evidence. Not long before he died, the great sceptical philosopher A. J. Ayer underwent such an experience, and wrote about it in the *Sunday Telegraph*.[8] When he pondered the meaning of that experience, he rejected any religious interpretation. He argued that a proof of an afterlife would not be proof of a deity, and that all the evidence might show is that the human brain was more complex than originally thought. Near death is not death, and cannot be evidence for it. He concluded:

> My recent experiences have slightly weakened my conviction that my genuine death, which is due fairly soon, will be the end of me, though I continue to hope that it will be. They have not weakened my conviction that there is no god.

Exercises and Examination Advice

Make a list of the following terms in your notes and make sure you research them until you have a clear understanding of what each means:

Corporate experiences

Group hysteria

Social psychology

Toronto Blessing

Experiencing-As

The Character of Religious Experiences

Ineffability

Noetic quality

Transciency

Passivity

You should also be able to demonstrate a good understanding of the views of writers such as:

Thomas Hobbes

Bertrand Russell

William James

A useful exercise for this part of the course would be to discuss different kinds of experience and explore the question of what makes a religious experience different from other kinds of experience. You may also wish to explore why different people have the same experience and one will describe it as 'religious' while another would simply say it was a human experience. A good example of this would be the birth of a child which many will see as truly taking them closer to God while other may argue it is simply a moment when we feel fully human and that there is nothing of the divine about it.

Another exercise may be to discuss together alternatives to James' descriptions of religious experiences, coming up with a range of your own which may arguably be more useful for a twenty-first century approach.

You may then try:

'Only delusional people belief that their experiences could be religious.' Discuss.

Notes

1. Thomas Hobbes: *Leviathan*, Chapter 32.
2. Mark Wynn: *Emotional Experience & Religious Understanding*, Cambridge, 2005.
3. Ludwig Wittgenstein (1958) *Philosophical Investigations* (OUP), p. 194.
4. Perhaps most fully in: *God and the Universe of Faiths*, Chapter 3.
5. Vincent Brümmer (2008) *What Are We Doing When We Pray?* (Ashgate), pp. 85–7
6. Bantam
7. Moody, R. (1977) *Reflections on Life After Life: More Important Discoveries in the Ongoing Investigation of Survival of Life After Bodily Death.* (New York: Bantam).
   Moody, R. (1999) *The Last Laugh: A New Philosophy of Near-Death Experiences, Apparitions, and the Paranormal.* (Hampton Roads Publishing Company).
8. 'What I saw when I was dead . . .', *Sunday Telegraph* (28th August 1988), reprinted with minor amendments as 'That Undiscovered Country', *The Meaning of Life and Other Essays* (London: Wiedenfield and Nicholson, 1990), pp. 198–204, followed by 'Postcript to a Postmortem' which appeared in the *Spectator*, (15th October 1988), reprinted in the same collection, pp. 205–8.

Revelation and Scripture 7

Introduction

For many religious believers, the surest form of experience is their encounter with God in scripture, whether in the Christian Bible, the Holy Koran or in some other revelatory document. But, if what has been said about religious language is correct, it would follow that the words of scripture are human words, understood in human ways. This would be so, even if, as believers hold, God is communicating truths about himself. Whatever he might have to tell us must be communicated in human language, for that is all we can understand.

This thought makes us aware of difficulties. Suppose God is timeless, or, perhaps, outside time. God may be outside time, but we as humans experience life *within* time. For us, our lives are tensed, that is, we have past, present and future. In the present we are aware of our immediate present moving into the past, just as our future expectations become present realities, then part of our past. We cannot but experience ourselves as beings within time. And our language is created by us to reflect that reality as we know it. But if God is timeless, it would not be like that to God – the grammar of God would be different. God in the Bible looks forward to events, looks back at others and sometimes becomes angry at a given state of affairs. The God of the writers of

Scripture is one who is with his people in the time process. But suppose that God in himself is outside that process. Any communications he has with us will be in our grammar, not what Sir Michael Dummett has called the 'tense of timelessness'. If God wants to communicate with us in sentences, he will have to do so in the language we speak, with human tenses. And the words within those tenses will be human words which we can understand. God's words would not be – could not be – absolutely literal when describing God. We understand a word such as 'love' on the basis of human experience of love – only that can give the word any sense. But, we are told that God's love surpasses human understanding. If he tells us that he loves us, we cannot give just our meaning to the term.

For this reason, even if, as some believe, Scripture is 'the Word of God', even the 'words of God', we cannot straightforwardly say that its meaning will be plain. The danger of doing so – in religious terms – would be idolatry, in the sense of making God in our own image.

Biblical Criticism

This is why scholars of the past were so aware of the dangers. In the Middle Ages, scripture was not taken as literally as it sometimes was in post-Reformation times. As we saw in our AS book, Origen, around 200 AD, stressed the allegorical nature of scripture, demonstrating that Genesis could not be literally true, but signified meta-phorically a deep religious truth about the nature of the world and God's relationship with it.

In the Middle Ages, especially following the growth of Scholasticism, scholars used a subtle, four-fold technique in their interpretation of the Bible. A full exegesis involved the following pattern, with the aim of bringing out the full meaning of the text:

1. The *literal* sense simply explained the text, especially the 'historical' accounts.
2. The *allegorical* sense referred to the true spiritual meaning.
3. The *tropological* sense brought out the moral and pastoral meaning.
4. The *anagogical* sense dealt with eschatology (the last things, such as judgment and eternal life) and the nature of the heavenly realities.

At its best, this proved a most sensitive way of dealing with the different demands of commentary on texts of different intent. By the fifteenth century, however, it was often used mechanistically: scholars would try to tease each type of meaning not only from passages but from phrases and individual words. The result was that editions of the Bible tended to be swamped by glossary and commentary.

Scholars such as Erasmus of Rotterdam (c.1466–1536), known as Humanists, argued even in the sixteenth century that Christians were in danger of losing the original meaning of Scripture. A way to think of this is to think of the word 'house'. Suppose we translate that word into Mongolian or another tongue. The word might have the same meaning, but the mental picture of a house would be different for a Mongolian in a yurt to someone living in a detached villa in Surbiton. The genius of Erasmus was to recognize that if we wanted to know precisely what Jesus meant, we needed to look beyond what we mean by a word to what Jesus meant by it. To do this meant trying to retranslate the New Testament from the oldest available sources to get back to the original meaning. The Reformers saw the Bible as having been falsified in the teaching of the Catholic Church and sought to return to the purity of earlier time. Their cry was '*sola fides, sola scriptura*', which we may translate as 'faith alone, scripture alone'.

To many at the Reformation, what was needed was for the believer to engage directly with the word of scripture. This was achievable partly through translation into the vernacular, whether in the great German Bible of Luther or versions such as those of Coverdale or the later King James Version. This enterprise was made possible above all by the development of the printing press. Coupled with the development of private spaces in houses and the habit of silent reading developed from the twelfth century, the mechanisms were in place for a faith based on direct, personal encounter with scripture as, for many, the principal way of experiencing the Word of God.

There was not complete agreement between the Reformers on how Scripture might be read. Martin Luther believed in close textual reading – he was perhaps the inventor of the printed handout as a teaching tool. He had printed for his students wide-spaced pages of biblical text, the gaps being for their notes. For him, the key to religious understanding was – as Catholics did – to see the Old Testament as prelude to the fullness of Christ's message in the New. Luther did not deny the significance of reason or Church tradition, but these were to be in service to Scripture and faith. John Calvin, on the other hand, tended to treat the whole Bible as 'The Word of God': each section was equal in its significance. This led to a perhaps more legalistic approach to Scripture (Calvin was by training a lawyer, not a theologian). The Roman Catholic Church, meanwhile, retained a two–tiered approach. Scripture was from God, but was mediated and interpreted by the Church's teaching authority, on the basis of Jesus' charge to Peter ('Thou art Peter, and on this rock I will build my church').

In the nineteenth century, there were huge advances in Biblical interpretation, especially in Germany. Part of this grew out of advances in archaeology. More knowledge was available about Biblical times, and this affected understanding. A deeper knowledge of history created a climate in which it seemed possible to go behind the words on the page to find a deeper meaning. This led to new types of criticism, principally:

- *Higher Criticism*, associated with – among others – Friedrich Schleiermacher (1768–1834), Ludwig Feuerbach (1804–72) and David Friedrich Strauss (1808–74). The concern of this was largely to bring a rational approach to scripture, to understand its nature as a body of human texts. Such an approach is offensive to many believers.
- *Historical Criticism* looks to the historical method of dating a specific piece of writing, attempting to understand the background against which a book of the Bible was written. Such knowledge is designed to deepen understanding, by, for example, showing the significance of events described in the text and making use of archaeological discoveries.
- *Literary Criticism* considers the forms, structures and themes in Scripture, asking whether something should be understood as poetry or narrative etc. It functions in much the same way as any other type of literary criticism, looking at devices such as symbol, tone and patterns of language. This often involves considerable linguistic skill, looking at the original grammar and forms.
- *Source Criticism* deals with the sources of scripture. It asks what collections of writings a scribe might have used.
- *Form Criticism* uses both historical and literary criticism, looking at the literary forms used by the writers to determine the intention of the writers. They will pay attention to how a particular text recurs throughout the Bible, perhaps recast in slightly different forms. Famous exponents include Hermann Gunkel (1862–1932) and Sigmund Moinkel (1884–1965).
- *Tradition*. Criticism considers how different traditions are passed down through the centuries during which the Bible was written.
- *Redaction Criticism* considers how a given part of the Bible reached its final form – it considers in depth questions of how texts were edited.
- *Textual Criticism* – sometimes called *Lower Criticism* – concentrates on questions of the meaning of original wording a scripture. Hebrew is an ambiguous language, largely because of a lack of vowels in its written form, and we lack original copies of the books of the Bible. Miscopying happens, and individual communities sometimes adapted passages to fit their own needs. The concern of the textual critic is to recover as closely as may be the original text.

These different forms of criticism led to attempts to discover what the Christ of history might really have been like: this was the effort of Albert Schweitzer (1875–1965) in *The Quest of the Historical Jesus* (1906), in which, based on the synoptic Gospels (Mark, Matthew and Luke, called *synoptic* because they are assumed to be based on a common collection of sources, mainly recalled sayings of Jesus, usually known as Q, or *Quelle* – which, in German, means 'source' or 'spring'), he argued that Jesus came only gradually during a short ministry of less than a year to recognize himself as Messiah. To save his followers from the evils of the last days, he permitted himself to suffer the Passion. This view remains controversial.

We saw, in our consideration of myth, how Rudolf Bultmann developed Biblical Criticism in demythologizing the Bible. His pupil, Fritz Buri, has gone even further. Where Bultmann argued that we need to strip away the layers of myth to reach the *kerygma*, the true message of Jesus, Buri has argued for dekerygmatizing the scriptures. This, critics argued would leave us with no more than that Jesus lived and died. Indeed, for Buri, there was little specifically Christian in religious faith.

Such approaches led some to a denial of Biblical scholarship. Most significant was the rise of Fundamentalism, a twentieth-century development which can be seen as a denial not only of new scholarly methods but also of the challenge to faith posed by modern science. The new Fundamentalism insisted on the literalness and inerrancy of the Bible in ways not previously encountered in scholarship. The term 'Fundamental-ist' came first from the Niagara Bible Conference (1878–97) which defined certain notions as 'fundamental to faith'. A set of 12 books published in 1910 by Milton and Lyman Steward was known as 'The Fundamentals', and the 1910 *General Assembly of the Presbyterian Church*, an American body, declared five 'fundamentals' of faith:

- The inspiration of the Bible by the Holy Spirit and the absolute accuracy of Scripture.
- The virgin birth of Christ.
- The belief that Christ's death was the atonement for sin.
- The bodily resurrection of Christ.
- The historical reality of Christ's miracles.

For most people, it is the first of these beliefs that constituted Fundamentalism. Although straightforward, the Fundamentalist move creates many problems. There are discrepancies between the gospels. In Mark, for example, both thieves at Calvary abuse Jesus – the story of Dismas, the good thief, appears as a later addition. There are discrepancies in accounts of Jesus' miracles, and there are questions about whether the parables are to be taken literally. Teachings in parts of the Old Testament appear not to correspond precisely with some of Jesus' comments in the New. It seems impossible to approach the Bible without an overlay of interpretation – to say the Bible is literally true is itself an interpretation. The Bible is not a self-authenticating document – nowhere does it command literal acceptance of itself. The question then arises about the authority by which Fundamentalists can make their assertions. Some critics go further, arguing that in practice Fundamentalists pick and choose which parts of Scripture they find most appealing, which is at odds with the fundamental notions of Biblical inerrancy – they have no authority for doing so. Others go so far as to accuse them of bibliolatry – worship of the Bible instead of God.

A common way to see these approaches to Scripture is to divide believers into:

- *Literalists*, who treat every sentence as true and cognitive;
- *Conservatives*, who accept the general message as from God – thus treating Scripture as the Word of God – but accepting the role of Biblical scholarship. Such an approach does not argue that every word is factually true, but believes the message to be authentic – this is roughly the position of the Roman Catholic Church, which has never taken the Bible literally;
- *Liberals*, who take a very open approach to Scripture, seeing it as fundamentally a human document, to be interpreted in the light of our times. This approach encompasses a whole range of possible approaches, from those of Bultmann and Buri to more traditional ideas represented by scholars such as Maurice Wiles.

Propositional Approaches to Revelation, Faith and Scripture

Philosophers tend to look to the traditions of Propositional and Non-Propositional views of both faith and Scripture.

A *propositional* view holds that the content of faith is a series of truths – a set of propositions – revealed by God. Faith is a matter of assent to those truths.

What those truths may be will vary from tradition to tradition. A Roman Catholic would see those truths as laid down in Scripture, in the Creeds and in the doctrines of the Church, with Faith the willing acceptance of these as true. A traditional Protestant might argue that what mattered were the truths found in Scripture, the Creeds and the Confessions of the Reformers, such as Philip Melanchthon. An evangelical Christian might argue that faith meant accepting the literal truth of the Bible. Islam generally takes a propositional view of the Holy Koran.

In the propositional tradition, there is a tendency to make a distinction between *natural* and *revealed* theology. Natural theology deals with those truths about which are knowable through the unaided human intellect, such as that he exists, that he is creator and so on. Revealed theology concerns those truths about God which are only knowable through God's special revelation, such as the Trinity or the divine nature of Jesus. This distinction is generally rejected by those who hold a non-propositional view.

In relation to the Bible, many in this tradition treat what they might call 'The Word of God' as 'the words of God'. After all, what is in the Bible is God's revelations – a series of propositions – about himself.

Non-propositional Approaches to Revelation, Faith and Scripture

As, the name implies, on this view, the content of revelation is not a series of truths – propositions – which God has taught us, but rather the self-revelation of God. God reveals himself to humankind, with faith being the human response to God.

A good way to think of this is to look at the propositional approach as 'Belief *that* . . . such and such a proposition is true', whereas non-propositional faith is 'Belief *in*. . . .' In our own experience we know what it means to believe *in* someone: it is an expression of trust in that person, and it is also a commitment to the significance of that person. In involving a commitment, it is different from a simply intellectual assent. When I assent to the proposition that Everest is the highest mountain, it is matter of my mind: it doesn't change my life or demand any particular commitment of my heart and soul. But to commit myself to the personal demands of another human being is thoroughly life-changing. It is perhaps worth noticing that when we commit to a person, we do so because something about the character of that person strikes us as worthy of our trust, even though we may know very few of the truths *about* her. (You might reflect on how this thought relates to Mitchell's parable of the partisan).

An excellent way of thinking about this type of revelation may be found in the work of the Jewish theologian, Martin Buber (1878–1965). In his *Ich und Du* (1922), (translated as *I and Thou*, T. T. Clarke, 1937), Buber plays on a distinctive personal pronoun – *du* is an intimate and personal usage, like *tu* in French, used for 'you' to members of the immediate family or to particularly close friends. ('Thou' once served the same function in English, hence the title of the English translation.) Buber distinguishes between 'I-It' relations, which we may have with an inanimate object, such as my relationship with my cheese-grater or my copy of *Kennedy's Shorter Latin Primer*, and *I-Thou* relationships, such as those with my family. The change is not simply one of grammar, but the different grammatical usages indicate a change of relationship. I do not speak directly to my cheese-grater, I have no dialogue with it, give it no orders, ask it no questions, never pay heed to its thoughts, feelings or needs. In my school days, I occasionally directed rude words at *Kennedy's Shorter Latin Primer*, but had no dialogue with it, and cared not a jot for its feelings. But with a person, everything changes: feelings matter, there is the interplay of relationship, we are affected in our inmost being – and there is response: they answer back.

Many of the traditional ways of dealing with questions of God are of the 'Does God exist?', 'What is God Like?' form. Those are 'I-It' questions, not dissimilar to asking whether the Loch Ness Monster exists. But if the question is different – *Who art Thou?*, rather than *What is He?*, then the entire discourse is changed and we are involved in a different type of question.

From this understanding, we can understand why theologians who have adopted non-propositional approaches, such as Emil Brunner (1889–1966), have rejected natural theology: it asks the wrong type of question.

The non-propositional approach involves a different approach to the Bible. No longer is it the 'Word of God', at least in the sense of being 'the words of God'. Non-propositional thinkers often point to the opening of St John's Gospel:

In the beginning was the Word, and the Word was with God, and the Word was God.

This clearly does not mean: 'In the beginning was the Bible, and the Bible was with God, and the Bible was God.' In scripture, the Word of God was Christ himself, giving himself to the world. On this view, the Bible is not the word of God, but an indispensable guide to the Word. The Gospels are a witness of faith, written by those who accepted the Word as the Word, in true belief. So, the Scripture becomes not an infallible witness, but rather an authentic understanding – by humans – of the event of revelation. This is why, at Nicaea in 325, the assembled fathers of the church accepted only some writings as authentic when constructing the New Testament. (Modern scholarship has largely endorsed the authenticity of their choices.) The test they applied was that they must come from the circle of Jesus and be written from the perspective of faith. The historian, Josephus, who wrote about Jesus, did not do so as one who accepted his self-revelation, so his work has no place in the New Testament.

An advantage of the approach just given is that it deals with the issue of how people could be described as believers in the years before the Bible as we know it existed. In Christian terms, they believed *in* Christ. The issue is somewhat different for Islam, as the writing of the Holy Koran was the beginning of their faith – in Christianity, scripture to a degree *followed* the beginnings of the religion.

Problems and a Word of Caution

The obvious issue with non-propositional approaches are that we perhaps cannot take away a significant part of the propositional approach. Part of my reason for believing *in* you is *that* you are such-and-such a person. Mitchell's partisan believes *in* the character of the Stranger, but he also believes *that* the Stranger is indeed the head of the Resistance. In the same way, the believer who believes *in* Jesus, believes *that* he is the Son of God.

We might note also that we may lose faith *in* someone if we discover *that* his self-description was untrue. If the Stranger was demonstrated to be lying, and he was indeed a traitor, the partisan, unless insane, would cease to trust in him. Faith always involves certain beliefs about the object of faith as well as any personal relationship. We might also remember that we are sometimes capable of fooling ourselves into mistaken beliefs about people, and we are only aware of our error in the light of facts, which are always propositions.

Perhaps we should say that for most people, the reality of faith is a mixture of several ways of believing, and that what leads to differences between believers is differences of emphasis. Evangelicals may believe that the Bible is the Word of God, but believe no less fervently in Jesus as personal Saviour and their relationship with him. At the Second Vatican Council, the assembled bishops proclaimed:

> In His goodness and wisdom God chose to reveal Himself and to make known to us the hidden purpose of His will (see Eph. 1:9) by which through Christ, the Word made flesh, man might in the Holy Spirit have access to the Father and come to share in the divine nature (see Eph. 2:18; 2 Peter 1:4). Through this revelation, therefore, the invisible God (see Col. 1; 15, 1 Tim. 1:17) out of the abundance of His love speaks to men as friends (see Ex. 33:11; John 15:14–15) and lives among them (see Bar. 3:38), so that He may invite and take them into fellowship with Himself. This plan of revelation is realized by deeds and words having in inner unity: the deeds wrought by God in the history of salvation manifest and confirm the teaching and realities signified by the words, while the words proclaim the deeds and clarify the mystery contained in them. By this revelation then, the deepest truth about God and the salvation of man shines out for our sake in Christ, who is both the mediator and the fullness of all revelation. *Dei Verbum*, Chapter 1, 1965.

One cannot quickly disentangle propositional from non-propositional elements – both are present. God both reveals himself and utters sentences to be believed.

The distinction between propositional and non-propositional approaches is theologically and philosophically valuable, but it is not the whole story of faith as lived.

Exercises and Examination Advice

Make a list of the following terms in your notes and make sure you research them until you have a clear understanding of what each means:

Scholasticism

Literal sense

Allegorical sense

Tropological sense

Anagogical sense

The Reformation

Higher Criticism

Historical Criticism

Literary Criticism

Source Criticism

Form Criticism

Tradition

Redaction Criticism

Textual Criticism

Propositional

Non-propositional

You should also be able to demonstrate a good understanding of the views of writers such as:

Erasmus of Rotterdam

Martin Luther

Martin Buber

Thomas Aquinas

A useful exercise to understand different kinds of biblical criticism is to look at the way the same story is told by different newspapers on the same day. This is particularly useful if it is a political story. You will not only be able to see through the information used and the 'spin' put on it and the political leanings of the editorial staff on that paper. The level of language used will demonstrate something about the expected readership of the newspaper. If you use the skills gained from studying redaction criticism and literary criticism it can be an interesting activity to look at a number of versions of the same story and work backwards to explore; who was it written for, what kind of people were writing it, what parts of each version did they choose to emphasize, what answers were they possibly looking for before they started writing the stories? The most obvious is the day after a by-election when every party has won! However, that may be too easy; a harder alternative may be to take some stories about education or unemployment or single parents and see what you can learn from them.

This should, we hope, give you an idea of just how hard it is to get into the minds of writers who were writing in different cultures two millennia and more ago.

Then try and answer the following question:

'As the Deity will always be a mystery, revelation is impossible.' Discuss.

Miracles 8

Introduction

Perhaps the miracle can be understood as a particularly dramatic type of religious experience. Discussion of miracles is, for many, central to the understanding of faith. For some, miracles are proof of the truth of, as well as the power of, God. In Christianity, at least one miracle, the resurrection, lies at the centre of people's belief. For the non-believer, miracle claims are an obstacle to belief. Tales of walking on water, turning water to wine, mysteriously multiplying loaves, seem at best mere mythical survivals, unworthy of belief in a scientific age, or, at worst, absurd, with belief in them a sign of childishness and weakness of mind.

For the believer, miracles bring problems. There is an ever-present danger of reducing religious truth to a series of magic tricks, with Jesus or a prophet as a master-magician. More persistently, there are question of why a miracle there, but not here – why boost a party where some had probably already had enough to drink, but do nothing to free the Jews from Roman rule? In our own times, why make a statue weep, but do nothing for the hungry and persecuted in Darfur, or heal this sick person at Lourdes but not the many thousands of other sick and devout pilgrims?

Nor is there agreement about what a miracle is. For St Thomas Aquinas – who does not devote much of his theological speculation to the subject – there are two key aspects:

> Two things may be considered in miracles. One is that which is done: this is something which surpasses the faculty of nature . . . The other thing is the purpose for which miracles are done, namely the manifestation of something supernatural, and for this reason they are commonly called *signs*: but on account of some excellence they receive the name of *wonder* or *prodigy*, as showing something from afar. *S.T.*, II, II, Q.178, a 1, r 3.

For Aquinas, the principal issue is God's purpose in using miracles – what they signify is more important than either the mechanics of how they come about or whether there are such things. For Aquinas, the critical issue is the question of discernment, that is, how to recognize true from false ones (perhaps done by demons, or the Anti-Christ[1]) accurately and how they are to be understood. But the signs that true miracles give are designed to tell us about God:

> . . . the Holy Ghost provides sufficiently for the Church in matters profitable for salvation, to which gratuitous graces are directed [by God]. Now, just as the knowledge which a man receives from God must be given to others through the gift of tongues and the grace of the word, so also the word uttered needs to be confirmed so that it is made believable. This is done by the working of miracles, according to Mark 16:20, 'And confirming the word with signs that followed': and reasonably so. For it is natural for man to arrive at the intelligible truth through its effects on our senses. Just as man led by his natural reason can arrive at some knowledge of God through His natural effects on the world, so he can achieve a degree of supernatural knowledge of the objects of faith by certain supernatural effects which are called miracles. *S.T.*, II, II, Q.172, a 1, c.

It therefore follows that for Aquinas a miracle teaches, and, of course, a miracle is always understood religiously. It is not simply a wonder, like an extraordinary magic trick, but a showing forth of God, teaching the world about him. As we shall see, much modern theological concern has been with the significance of miracles rather than their mechanics: in a sense, modern discussion has, within religious discourse, gone back to issues of meaning, rather than their ontological status. In this, perhaps religious discussion has followed modern philosophy in its movement away from questions of knowledge to questions of meaning.

Certainly, for an event to be called a miracle it has to be interpreted as a miracle. Certain experienced events are called miracles – sometimes very loosely, as when something like having a baby, or my finding my lost spectacles, is called a 'miracle'. These may be wonderful events, but they are not rare or unknown in the normal course of the world. But neither should we just dismiss this usage as mistaken. The birth of a child, though not perhaps my finding my spectacles, may surely be interpreted religiously, as a gift of God, a mystery of life, a manifestation of divine love blessing human love. It is the reception of the event which is the justification of the term.

R. F. Holland[2] is a modern exponent of such a view, arguing that miracles are coincidences religiously interpreted. He gives the example of a small boy playing on a railway track. He becomes stuck, and is saved from death only because the driver of the train collapses on to the dead man's handle, and thus the train has stopped. The boy's mother thinks the event miraculous – the sick driver might think otherwise.

But many religious believers believe that, though significance is central to the concept of miracle, they are actual interventions of God. Aquinas distinguished different types of miracles. In some cases, God does what nature could never do, at other times, he does things in a different order or more quickly than nature would. People recover from illnesses, but not in an instant. Sometimes God acts directly, at other times he might work through a saint. Underlying Aquinas' idea, there is a belief in the miracle as a kind of *intervention*.

David Hume on Miracles

The Dutch, Jewish philosopher, Baruch Spinoza, described miracles as a 'violation' of the laws of nature,[3] which might be open to question. For a Thomist, as we saw, a miracle need not violate nature's laws – it could be a speeding-up, slowing-down or reordering. But a similar definition was given by David Hume:

> A miracle is a violation of the laws of nature. . . . David Hume, *An Enquiry Concerning Human Nature*, Section X, 'Of Miracles', Part I.

He goes on to argue that:

> . . . as a firm and unalterable experience has established these laws, the proof against a miracle, from the very nature of the fact, is as entire as any argument from experience can possibly be imagined. Ibid.

At the heart of Hume's argument is an appeal to the *principle of induction*. This notion is based on the idea that we make scientific judgments based on many instances. For instance, we collect many instances of the sun rising in the morning, and then draw the general conclusion that 'the sun rises every day'. The more instances, the more probable the conclusion. Hume argues that this is the basis of science, and claims that it is highly rational to believe the highly probable, and highly irrational to believe the highly improbable. The point about a miracle is that it is by definition highly improbable – otherwise it would not *be* a miracle – and thus is not worthy of belief. The key to his argument is this:

A wise man . . . proportions his belief to the evidence. In such conclusions as are founded on an infallible experience, he expects the event with the last degree of assurance, and regards his past experience as a full *proof* of the future existence of that event . . . And as an uniform experience amounts to a proof, there is . . . a direct and full *proof*, from the nature of the fact, against the existence of any miracle; nor can such a proof be destroyed, or the miracle rendered credible, but by an opposite proof, which is its superior. Ibid.

It should be noticed at once that Hume is using the word 'proof' in a very idiosyncratic way. We understand a proof as demonstrating something beyond any possible doubt. But Hume is not taking the word to mean that – notice that he speaks rather of what wise men consider *as* proof. Otherwise, it would make no sense to speak of 'opposite proofs'. What Hume means by 'proof' is the best we can get from any observation – the highest probability.

Hume was fully aware that induction can never be certain. A careful examination of the *Enquiry* supports this reasoning:

All inferences from experience . . . are effects of custom, not of reasoning. . . . It is that principle alone which renders our experience useful to us, and makes us expect, for the future, a similar train of events with those which have appeared in the past. David Hume, *An Enquiry Concerning Human Nature*, Section V, 'Sceptical Solutions', Part I.

As a great number of views . . . concur in one event, they fortify and confirm it to the imagination, beget that sentiment which we call *belief*, and give its object preference above the contrary event, which is not supported by an equal number of experiments, and recurs not so frequently to the thought in transferring the past to the future. David Hume, *An Enquiry Concerning Human Nature*, Section V, 'Of Probability'.

In summary, then, Hume's case is:

1. The laws of nature are inductive probabilities;
2. The greater the number of observations the more highly probable they become;
3. They are as nearly certain as any understanding could possibly be as they are based on countless observations;
4. Miracles are, by definition, a breach of those highly probable laws of nature;
5. They are thus, by definition, highly improbable – the weight of evidence is against them;
6. It is irrational to believe the highly improbable as this is to believe against the weight of evidence;
7. Therefore it is irrational to believe in miracles.

Hume's Subsidiary Arguments

Hume supports his argument by further considerations, based on the notion that we are all familiar with the unreliability, because of ignorance, wickedness, drunkenness or honest error, of human reports. Any policeman will tell you of how perfectly honest witnesses give very different accounts of the same event. Human error is an everyday experience – miracles are not.

Hume makes four additional points:

1. No miracle in history has been attested by 'a sufficient number of men, of such unquestioned good-sense, education and learning, as to secure us against all delusion in themselves; of such undoubted integrity, as to place them beyond all suspicion of any design to deceive others . . .'[4]
2. Human beings love tales of the weird and miraculous, so there is a natural disposition to suspend disbelief and to accept whatever is said. We have firm evidence of people giving credence to fraudulent 'miracles', and people love to gossip and pass on tales, the more extreme, the better.
3. Belief in supernatural and miraculous events is found principally in ignorant and barbarous nations. If belief in miracles is found among advanced nations, it is only because it was handed down from ignorant and barbarous ancestors.
4. Every type of religion seems to have its own miracle claims, each demonstrating the truth of that religion. They cannot all be true and the religious claims cancel out each other, so no credence can be given to them.

Against these supporting arguments, various objections are possible.

It may be doubted that only ignorant and barbarous nations and people attest to miracles. Hume asserts his case without evidence. We might argue that the veracity of an observation is not determined by the educational level or social status of the witness: we do not debar those without A Levels from giving evidence in court on the grounds that they are incompetent to recount accurately what they saw. It could be argued that simplicity of mind adds credence to a statement – it is the clever mind which can be devious, the more fluent one more likely unconsciously to elaborate the tale. As for the argument that miracles may be found in all religions, it could be argued that God might wish to reveal himself in different ways through different religions.

We might draw attention to Richard Swinburne's thoughts on reports. He has recourse to two principles:

- *The principle of testimony*, which argues that people generally do tell the truth;
- *The principle of credulity*, which argues that therefore people should generally be believed unless there is good evidence to doubt them (such as drink, drugs or a history of dishonesty).

Of course, it does not follow from Swinburne's argument that we could just give credence to a given report of a miracle, which is a problem: one would want to know that *this* miracle is true, whether it be the Resurrection of Christ or a claimed miraculous healing. The question of whether a miracle really happened is a particular question, not a general one, and Swinburne's principles are inevitably general ones.

The Problem of Hume's Inductivism

Hume was aware that induction has its own problems, notably, the logical Problem of Induction. The problem is simply explained – the only proof we have that many instances of events giving us probable general conclusions is the many instances of events giving us probable general conclusions. The only evidence for induction is induction itself. This circularity is an issue, as it means that we cannot find external support for the principles on which the laws of nature depend.

But suppose the argument that we learn and make our scientific judgments on the basis of many repeated instances is itself erroneous? This was precisely the position adopted by Sir Karl Popper (1902–94). The notion of induction presupposes that we first collect many instances and *then* formulate our general principle. Popper argued that no one thinks like that. Our minds are not passive collectors of instances – we actively shape our world. Think of the caveman. He did not blindly record on the cave wall every time the sun rose, and after many generations say, 'we have now collected enough instances that we are probably in a position to formulate a general scientific principle.' For Popper, no one thinks that way: to do so is to be passive, like a camera set up at random, just recording everything that happens in front of it.

Popper, following the insight of Franz Brentano (1838–1917), accepts that the mind is *intentional*, that is, it seeks out features of the world and does not wait for the world to come to it. This is illustrated by Popper's telling a class to follow his instructions. He said, 'Observe!' The students naturally asked: 'Observe what?' – they could hardly record everything. When we look at the world, the mind naturally concentrates on one thing rather than another – we cannot just soak up everything in front of us. When I look at Tweazel (the cat who wrote much of this book in idle moments), I look at her, and though I am aware of them, I pay them little heed to things in the background. When I speak to someone, I look at that person – there is a great difference between what I *see* and what I am looking at. And our perception is always like that – we would probably go mad if it were not, and we treated everything with equal concentration.

Popper argues that when we perceive and draw our conclusions, we do not simply collect observations. Rather, we notice a feature of our experience and form an hypothesis. The man who walks past my gate each morning as I leave for work, causes me to hypothesize that he works at the college up the road. I form a hypothesis. Suppose my hypothesis is wrong, how would I test it? Perhaps he will walk by the college and instead turn into the public house at the end of that road. I know what would disprove my theory. For Popper, we first produce an hypothesis, deduce what would test its truth, then carry out the test. What we do not do is to wait until we have seen that man pass the gate every day for five years before saying 'I wonder if . . . '. We are curious creatures, and creators of hypotheses. If Hugh does not answer the telephone, I wonder what he is doing, not because I am nosey, but because as a human, I am a creator of theories.

But this is not all. If Popper is right, then we do not learn by induction, but there is a further consequence from Popper's notion of falsification. *High probability does not count in favour of a theory.* There are two reasons why this is so. Take the example of the sun rising each day. It has risen n billion times. In a million years, it will have risen a further 365 million or so times. But it is not more likely it will rise then – it is less likely. The sun will be much closer to extinction, if not already not extinct. That I have been alive for the last x years does not entail that it is more likely that I shall be alive in 50 years – it is less likely.

Nor is that all. For science to be informative, according to Popper, it has to be highly improbable. Consider two weather forecasts:

- It will rain, somewhere, some time.
- It will be raining in London at midday tomorrow.

The second is far more informative than the first, and far more likely to be wrong, as we saw in Chapter 4. If we seek high probability, we find ourselves with anodyne and practically worthless science.

If we apply this to the question of miracles, we can see that our miracles may be those key disconfirming instances. Faced with these, we can argue, as John Hick does, that perhaps our laws of nature are mistaken and they need to be reformulated – after all, it is the exception that disproves the rule. We might also argue that if miracles are exceptions to the laws of nature, we cannot argue, as Hume does, that *all* testimony clearly favours the uniformity of the laws of nature, for in the miracle accounts there is testimony that contradicts it. If we argue simply that *most* testimony favours the uniformity of those laws, then there is immediately room for the exception. Hume's position seems to be to deny the possibility of exception, which is itself to prejudge the conclusion.

Maurice Wiles on Miracles

Maurice Wiles (1923–2005), the distinguished Anglican theologian, considered a moderate liberal, was Regius Professor of Divinity at Oxford (later Emeritus), and for many years chaired the Church of England Doctrine Commission until he was removed by Archbishop Carey. Underlying all his works is a very a lively awareness of the presence of God behind the world, performing the single miracle of creation. There is also a profound awareness of the limits of language in the theological enterprise of comprehending that God.

His views on miracles are most famously contained in his 1986 Bampton Lectures, (published as *God's Action in the World*, SCM, 1986), but it is helpful to supplement his original points by other comments from his work. Perhaps most accessible is *Reason to Believe* (SCM, 1999).

Wiles points to the problems of defining a miracle. He considers the Humean approach of a miracle as 'a direct act of God that contravenes the laws of nature'. Rightly, he points out that the laws of nature are continually revisable (*Reason to Believe* p. 38), as we saw in our discussion of Hume. He shows that a miracle must not simply be a rare event – it has a religious dimension. He rehearses a number of objections close to Hume's subsidiary arguments about past times, unreliability of witness, misdescription etc. He grants that direct divine action cannot be dismissed as logically incoherent.

But his principal focus is on the theological significance of miracles. Given the problems of any account of miracles, it seems to him appropriate to ask in what sense Christian belief is dependent on accepting the objective reality of the miraculous as a direct intervention by God.

In *Reason to Believe*, he questions the place of miracle in Christian faith as a whole (p. 40). He argues that many biblical miracle stories, including the Virgin Birth, are legendary without any claim of historical accuracy. And they are not an essential element for the truth of Christian faith, as they are at least as questionable as the doctrines they are supposed to prove. He notes how Jesus himself refused to provide miraculous signs to prove his divine authority. In relation to miracles as answers to prayer, he points out that miracles are rare indeed while prayer unaccompanied by miracles lies at the heart of the Christian experience:

> The deeper the exploration into the practice of prayer, the less helpful does the concept of miracle appear. Ibid., p. 42.

This focus is perhaps more evidently theological than in *God's Action in the World*. In the earlier book, Wiles raises similar points about science but develops the moral issue of a God who intervenes on trivial matters but does nothing to prevent Hiroshima or Nagasaki.

> . . . to acknowledge even the possibility of miracle raises acute problems for theodicy. *God's Action in the World*, p. 66.

He notes the importance of miracle in the Christian faith and asks whether it is possible to understand it in a revised way. He points to the idea that the key point in miracles is rather in the spiritual significance than the outer happening, noting Origen's dictum that the transformation of human lives is 'greater work . . . than the physical miracles which Jesus did.'

A fundamental question, dealt with in both books, is what such a reading would mean for such fundamental aspects of Christian belief as the Incarnation and Resurrection. In the earlier book, Wiles pays close attention to Hans Küng's approach:

> Hans Küng, in his widely read work, *On Being a Christian*, asserts roundly that 'the raising of Jesus is not a miracle violating the laws of nature . . . not a supernatural intervention which can be located in space and time.' Ibid., p. 90.

In this book, Wiles is cautious in presenting his alternative explanation. In *Reason to Believe*, he presents a more detailed account, arguing that the traditional resurrection and ascension accounts are not straightforward, that any attempt to demonstrate the historical core of these stories is bound to fail. He notes that we read symbolically such phrases as 'sitting on the right hand of God' and that we need to read the entire accounts in a way more symbolic than has often been customary within the Christian tradition. He is not unaware of the difficulties of such an approach for many believers:

> The story of Christ's resurrection (which . . . is really part of the single story of death-and-resurrection) symbolises the conviction that wickedness, suffering and death do not have the final word about human life . . . This way of expressing the symbolic significance of the Christian story by-passes a number of the difficulties that many people feel about it, particularly the miraculous character of some of its most prominent features. . . . There are those who will see it as a very watered-down version of what they understand the traditional faith to be. But it is no humanist platitude, and certainly far from the scepticism that often vies with credulity for the souls of men and women today. It makes strong claims, some of which conflict with our common sense assumptions about the world. *Reason to Believe* p. 46.

Here we seem to return to the Thomist emphasis on meaning rather than the mechanics of miracles. But many Christians would find in Wiles – as he acknowledges – a denial of events which they place at the heart of their own faith.

Exercises and Examination Advice

Make a list of the following terms and make sure you research them until you have a clear understanding of what each means:

Miracles

Proof

Inferences from experience

Probability

Subsidiary Arguments

Veracity

The principle of testimony

The principle of credulity

Inductivism

You should also be able to demonstrate a good understanding of the views of writers such as:

St Thomas Aquinas

R. F. Holland

David Hume

Baruch Spinoza

Richard Swinburne

Sir Karl Popper

John Hick

Maurice Wiles

Hans Küng

There are many angles from which this topic may be approached. One of them could be to explore actual accounts of miracles which have been reported in the present day or historically. You could, in groups, discuss a set of criteria by which the reliability of evidence could be assessed. You might, for example, try to make use of the kinds of questions that Hume would have wanted to ask, keeping in mind that he was not saying, with certainty, that miracles were impossible, rather that they were highly unlikely. Is he being fair, for example, in suggesting that many reports of miracles come from people we may naturally judge to be unreliable?

Alternatively, you could explore the issues raised by the views of Maurice Wiles; perhaps listing all the way his suggestion that a God who cures and helps some but fails to help the majority of those who find themselves in need of His aid, makes Him a God not worthy of worship.

Then you could try this question:

'Miracles are the least likely of events.' Discuss.

Notes

1. *S.T.*, II, II, Q172, a 1, r 3.
2. R. F. Holland (1965) 'The Miraculous', *American Philosophical Quarterly* 2: pp. 43–51.
3. B. Spinoza, *Tract.Theol.Polit.*, vi.
4. David Hume, *An Enquiry Concerning Human Nature*, Section X, 'Of Miracles', Part II.

The Divine Attributes 9

Introduction

This chapter, while having some discrete sections, also has a number of threads which link to and demonstrate the importance of many of the aspects of philosophy you have already studied. So, for example, it is important to keep in mind while we are exploring God's attributes that the language we are using is not without its own complications; and that, as is often the case in philosophy, the more you tie down the answer to one question, the more problems that are raised for other responses to problems within the threads we are discussing. The best way to make this clear is to start on the first topic, much of which will not be finished until the next chapter.

Eternity

To understand what it means to say that God is eternal, we need to be clear what we mean by the term 'God'. Is the term God describing a simple, in the platonic sense, divine entity? It is implicit in the philosophies of Plato and Aristotle that God must be outside and separate from both space and time and therefore unaffected by either. This doctrine, also found in St Thomas Aquinas, and earlier in the Fourth Lateran Council, states that God is not composed or divisible by any physical or metaphysical means. The term 'Simplicity of God' simply means that God is not made up of parts. This teaching is applied to our understanding of God's entire nature. His being, nature and substance is that of complete simplicity. The properties attributed to God, which are the main topic of this chapter, eternity, omnipotence, omniscience and omnipresence are not seen as contradicting this teaching of simplicity because each property is a different way of looking at the infinite active being of God from our human and limited perspective.

In its absolute sense, the term 'eternal' is often taken to mean infinite duration, just as 'omnipresence' may be taken to mean infinite presence. It is, however, more accurate to say that eternal means a duration without limits whether actual or imagined, without succession (that is, without one thing following another) and without end. It is therefore impossible to measure eternity: it is, as we will explore in the next chapter, an everlasting present.

Human beings experience time as a succession of moments and therefore find it nearly impossible to conceive of eternity in any other way apart from a duration indefinitely extended from the present moment in two directions. So we speak of eternity in terms of a past and a future, somewhat similar to how we conceive time, as past, present or still future. And, when we are discussing God, we are faced with a serious problem. Our grammar is tensed – that is, all our sentences are framed with verbs (remember that a sentence must have a verb), but all our verbs presuppose the kind of succession we are talking about here. Just as our experience has past, present and future, so do our verbs ('I ran', 'I run', 'I will run'). We try to express God in our language, as we have no other and no way of experiencing any other. What we mean by describing God as eternal in this sense is taking us beyond the limits of the language we are using to express the idea.

This idea of eternity as an unchanging present, without beginning or end, comprehending all of time, and a God who experiences all of time as a simultaneous moment will be considered in much more detail in the next chapter.

We, however, perceive God to be acting in a finite fashion; first purposing and then acting, first promising or threatening and then acting on his promise, and so forth. In the Bible we find God intimately concerned with history, with his people Israel and interacting with the nascent Christian community. But other parts of scripture are at odds with this; for He who inhabits eternity infinitely transcends our understanding (Isaiah 57:15). His eternity, therefore, leads us to believe that His immensity and infinity gives Him an altogether different nature from ours.

Any language we then use to try to talk about God will always be limited and fall short of describing a Being who is ultimately a mystery. As I said above, while we can solve some problems associated with each attribute, we almost inevitably create others as we go along.

Omnipotence

This attribute of God is probably the most well known both inside and outside philosophical circles. It is one of the most important concepts from the triad of beliefs which give us the problem of evil. If God were not described as omnipotent, then the problem of evil would presumably be solved. It is a problem because Christians claim to believe in a God who can do anything, but who, when faced with the appalling evils that visit the world, does apparently nothing. In its simplest definition it is the belief held by most monist faiths that God is 'all-powerful'. By now you will have studied enough philosophy to know that nothing is ever that simple. Richard Dawkins, in his book *The God Delusion*, neatly highlights the problem I have been alluding to; he says:

> Incidentally, it has not escaped the notice of logicians that omniscience and omnipotence are mutually incompatible. If God is omniscient, he must already know how he is going to intervene to change the course of history using his omnipotence. But that means he can't change his mind about his intervention, which means he is not omnipotent. Richard Dawkins: *The God Delusion*, Bantam, 2006, p. 78.

This kind of criticism appears to be of the '*God can't make a square circle*' or '*God can't make a stone so heavy He cannot lift it*' kind. It is clear that we will not get very far with this kind of discussion if we try to create illusory limitations 'in God' which are really limitations of our language and our ability to describe Him accurately. However, that is not to say that the language is meaningless.

So what do Christians really mean when they say that God is omnipotent? First, we need to say that it is generally believed that God can do anything which is logically possible. A good way to unpack these ideas is to compare the views of Descartes and Aquinas who held differing views on how we should understand 'omnipotence'.

Descartes described omnipotence as the ability to do absolutely anything. This led Descartes to argue for a God who can do the logically impossible; he would need to be able to make square circles, and also make $2 + 2 = 5$.

Thomas Aquinas proposed a narrower safer idea of what might be meant by omnipotence. He described God as being able to do *anything possible*; so, looking at scripture He can part the Red Sea, and he can restore the Lazarus to life, but Aquinas' God cannot violate the laws of logic and mathematics. Aquinas argued that a notion such as a 'square circle' is literally meaningless. As it is a contradiction, it is nothing but words – an empty concept which refers to no logically possible state of affairs.

To say something is possible makes sense only if it is indeed logically possible. If it is not logically possible, then it is nothing – and there would be nothing to achieve.

If you accept the Cartesian definition of omnipotence, then Dawkins', or any other attempt for that matter, to disprove God's existence using logic is doomed to failure. If you believe in a God who can do the logically impossible, then you have to believe that he can both create a stone so heavy that he cannot lift it, and yet still lift it. Clearly there is an explicit contradiction in this statement, but so what? On this understanding of omnipotence, God can make contradictions reality.

The more popular understanding of omnipotence, proposed by Aquinas, survives the paradox of the stone in a different way. If we can assume that God as defined by Aquinas exists, then he is a being who is capable of lifting any stone. A stone that is so heavy that God cannot lift it then it becomes an impossible object. We need to say this, because Aquinas has defined omnipotence for God by saying that He is able to do anything possible, but not anything impossible, and creating a stone that God cannot lift is something impossible. In this way to the question 'Can God create a stone to heavy for him to lift?', Aquinas can answer 'No' without undermining his believe in an omnipotent God.

One other, final approach to this problem would be to say that *within* the universe God has created he does not have the power to do just anything. Using the word 'almighty', rather than omnipotent, Peter Vardy puts it this way:

> To call God Almighty, therefore, is to recognise the ultimate the ultimate dependence of the universe and all things within it on God. It is to recognise God's creative and sustaining power. However, it specifically does not mean that God has total power to do anything He wishes. God is limited by the universe he has chosen to create. . . . This limitation does not, however, lessen God in any significant way. It is rather a recognition of God's wish to create a universe in which human beings can be brought into a loving relationship with him. Peter Vardy: *The Puzzle of Evil*, Fount, 1992, **124**.

Omniscience

A literal definition of this word would be to say that it means all-knowing; however, when we apply the word to God it has a number of nuances which need to be borne in mind. Arthur Conan Doyle used the word when he had Sherlock Holmes say of his brother Mycroft:

'All other men are specialists, but his specialism is omniscience.'

I do not think that Conan Doyle was suggesting that Mycroft was God-like in his knowledge, just that he seemed to retain a great deal of information and had a particular skill at processing it. When we talk of God being 'omniscient', we tend to mean much more. One of the problems which arise from this 'more' that God knows may limit our freedom, as how can we be free and God know in advance what we are going to do. One of the solutions to this is to say that God knows timelessly; however, as the next chapter is dedicated to resolving this particular problem, we need to look in this section more specifically at the meaning of this attribute for an everlasting, rather than timeless, God.

One of the main issues for an everlasting God would be whether he can know the future. If something has not yet happened, how can he know that it will? Richard Swinburne attempts to get round this problem by describing a God who knows everything which can possibly be known but maintains that this does not include knowledge of the future. He would argue that if we start from a position of human freedom, then we cannot believe in a God who knows our future without sacrificing our freedom. As a Scot, I am well aware of all that William Wallace and others had to say about the importance of freedom and everything else being taken away before we willingly sacrifice our freedom. Theologically this is equally important as the Christian understanding of our relationship with God is crucially a loving one, which, without freedom, would be meaningless.

One last aspect of this word worthy of exploration is the question of whether or not a Being who is omniscient has the capacity or need to learn. In the Bible, a famously contradictory collection of books, we are told by one of the writers of the book of Isaiah that God has never learned nor needed to learn anything from anyone. The prophet says:

> Who hath directed the Spirit of the Lord, or being his counsellor hath taught him? With whom took He counsel, and who instructed him, and taught him in the path of judgment, and taught him knowledge, and showed to him the way of understanding.

In the same way St Paul says:

> For who hath known the mind of the Lord? Or who hath been his counsellor?

Both Paul and Isaiah are saying that God has never learned and the implication of this is that he will never need to learn either. It may at this point be worth thinking of an earlier thread in the book, namely the idea that the apophatic way is the only way to a solution here. So in writing about the attributes of God, it could be argued that it is easier to say what God isn't than what God *is*. Our minds find it much easier to understand what God isn't, but our minds would seem to be too limited or even fragile to understand the mystery that is God.

Omnibenevolence

The concept of omnibenevolence has its roots in two different but related ideas about God: one being that God is perfect and the other that God is believed to be morally good. These beliefs lead to the understanding that God must be in possession of perfect goodness. Christianity locates the support for this belief in the Old Testament:

> As for God, his way is perfect: the word of the Lord is tried: he is a buckler to all those that trust in him.

This is just one of many quotations from sacred scriptures which support this understanding of God. In the late nineteenth century, this view of God was restated by the first Vatican Council:

> The Holy, Catholic, Apostolic and Roman Church believes and acknowledges that there is one true and living God, Creator and Lord of Heaven and earth, almighty, eternal, immeasurable, incomprehensible, infinite in will, understanding and **every perfection**. Since He is one, singular, completely simple and unchangeable spiritual substance, He must be declared to be in reality and in essence, distinct from the world, supremely happy in Himself and from Himself, and inexpressibly loftier than anything besides Himself which either exists or can be imagined.

Any philosophers who have accepted that God is logically necessary, such as St Anselm of Canterbury, also implicitly have to hold that if He was not morally perfect, that is, if God was merely a great being but nevertheless of finite benevolence, then the nature of his existence would be limited and not 'that than which nothing greater can be thought', because it would be possible to conceive of a being of greater benevolence.

While some religious traditions focus naturally on this interpretation of God's benevolence, other traditions see the concept as being more about God's justice, or indeed, in some cases, mercy. There is no obvious or necessary reason for preferring any one of these to any other; each is as philosophically coherent and consistent as another, and none of them needs empirical observations of God which would allow it to have any epistemological superiority.

This concept needs little more discussion here as, more than any of the other attributes. It is covered by many of the other threads throughout both of these books; the problem of evil, the problems with religious language, the Jewish understanding of Deity and so on.

STRETCH AND CHALLENGE

The concepts we looked at above are the only ones you will need to know to answer questions which might be set for the OCR papers. However, there are many more concepts which can be understood as attributes of God. One, which is more of a Greek concept than a Jewish one, is the idea that God is immutable, that is wholly unchangeable and unchanging. This is an idea which is worth researching and while you are doing so, ask yourself if God is indeed immutable is there any point in praying to him in a petitionary manner? Richard Swinburne has written interestingly on questions of immutability in: *The Coherence of Theism*, Oxford, pp. 212–17, contrasting 'stronger immutability', which means that God is effectively wholly disengaged from time (a Greek view), with 'weaker immutability' which is the notion that God's character does not change through eternity – part of that unchanging character could be an eternal desire for loving relationship with his creation, as a fixed disposition.

Exercise and Examination Advice

Make a list of the following terms in your notes and make sure you research them until you have a clear understanding of what each means:

Attribute

Eternity

Everlasting

Omnipotent

Omniscient

Omni-benevolent

An exercise which might be worth exploring in this area is the use of these words in fiction, through various media. For example, in the series *Star Trek: the Next Generation*, a race of supposedly 'omnipotent beings' called *Q* is supposed, using the idea of being who can do anything. In one episode, a *Q* has his power taken away. Do you think the writers were using the concept accurately or were they missing a key point about omnipotence?

Alternatively, you might explore the ideas about religious concepts in Graham Greene's, *The End of the Affair*. Here he creates a situation where an atheist ends up believing in God because he hates him, owing to God answering his lover's prayers, presumably benevolently.

There are many other examples which you may explore through internet search engines and perhaps share from your class's reading and film watching.

Finally you could try answering the following question:

To what extent can God be both all-powerful and all-knowing?

Time, Eternity and Divine Foreknowledge – The Boethian View

10

Introduction

Boethius was an important member of the court of Theodoric, arguably the most powerful man in Western Europe after the collapse of the Roman Empire around 500 AD. Theodoric had Boethius locked up when he became frightened that the Eastern Empire was plotting to overthrow him. *The Consolation of Philosophy* was written by Boethius while he was in prison to explain why he, who was believed to be a good Christian, had apparently been abandoned by fortune and God, and left to die by execution. This execution eventually, rather painfully, took place. The book is written as a dialogue between Boethius and 'Lady Philosophy'. The part of the dialogue we focus on here is about the extent to which Christians can, with integrity, believe in a God who rewards and punishes justly.

This time Boethius is addressing the problem that if God knows what we are going to do, then why do we not hold him, at least partly, responsible for the evil that men do? Unlike the approaches of Augustine and Irenaeus, he is arguing that God does not know in advance about human actions and therefore He cannot do anything about them. A reasonable summary of his method is to break it down into these parts:

- *To question what we mean by divine foreknowledge.*
- *To explore the meaning of eternity.*
- *To discuss two kinds of necessity – Simple and Conditional.*
- *To conclude that God rewards and punishes justly.*

Divine Foreknowledge

This is important as it is a direct challenge to the argument that if our behaviour is determined or even foreseen, then God has to take some responsibility for the evil actions brought about by humanity's free choices. To begin this discussion Boethius makes the following statement:

> Since we have shown that knowledge is not based on the thing known but on the nature of the knower, let us consider the nature of the Divine Being and what sort of knowledge it has.

Here it is worth exploring analogies of this idea such as Mozart, looking at a keyboard and just knowing how it worked, whereas a person born deaf will never know in the same way as Mozart. In the same way, this sentence will be understood at once by some:

> *You can split the world into 10, those who understand this and those who don't.*

Those who understand binary will make sense of this sentence immediately, but others will not be able to follow it without some explanation.

So, Boethius wants to argue that God's way of seeing the universe is very different from any human perception. His way of doing this is to say that all rational creatures judge the Divine Being to be eternal, so we should start by explaining the nature of eternity, for this will reveal to us the nature of the Divine Being and the capacity of divine knowledge. In other words, without understanding how God knows we cannot judge the effect of this knowledge. Boethius, working on the idea that God's knowledge is eternal, uses this definition:

> *Eternity is the **simultaneous** possession of boundless life which is made clearer by comparison with temporal things. This becomes clear when we consider temporal things: whatever lives in time lives only in the present, which passes from the past into the future, and no temporal thing has such a*

nature that it can simultaneously embrace its entire existence, for it has not yet arrived at tomorrow and no longer exists in yesterday.

I have highlighted the word 'simultaneous' as this is the most significant, but perhaps most difficult concept, but it is the key to the Boethian position. His argument is that while *we* are conditioned by time, and *to us* the future is not here yet and the past is gone, an unchangeable God is outside this universe and not affected by space or time. For God, all of the universe's 'moments' from the big bang through to however the universe ends, is one simultaneous moment. This means that at any moment of our life he does not see what we are going to do but he sees what we are doing.

A Useful Diversion

If you have some science students in the class with you, it may be worth spending some time getting them to help with a discussion of General Relativity. I say this mainly because it helps in thinking about this to break away from the perception of time as a constant unchanging influence on your life. Modern cosmology also helps by placing time firmly as part of the creation of the space–time continuum and therefore part of our universe, and not something which can affect God, as Boethius sees him, in any way.

In any discussion at this point, you may find yourself having trouble talking about God's knowledge in the present tense but it is worth persevering with this to make the point as clearly as possible. So, for example, you might try thinking about God's view like this. He sees:

A student being born, starting primary school, entering secondary school, starting A levels, receiving their results, going to university / work, marrying, having children, becoming a Grandparent and dying, all in the same moment.

It is in this sort of exercise that many of my students end up looking like the famous Munch painting, *The Scream.*

So at the end of this section, the key concept that you need to have understood is in Boethius' words:

Therefore, if you consider the divine foreknowledge through which God knows all things, you will conclude that it is not a knowledge of things in the future but a knowledge of an unchanging present.

In recent times, Professor Sir Michael Dummett has developed the idea that God thinks – that is, entertains propositions – in a tense of timelessness. The way we frame our sentences – the very stuff of our thoughts – is in terms of verbs that are always *tensed*, that is past, present, future, conditional and so on. Because of the way we are, we cannot construct our thoughts in a different way. But God is in no sense like us, and the mode of his thought will be shaped by the grammar of the divine state.

Two Kinds of Necessity

In introducing the idea of 'necessity', Boethius again compares the way we see things with the way that God sees things. He uses the word 'Providence' as opposed to 'Prevision' (which means 'seeing ahead') when explaining God's view of our existence; as God sees things not from our inferior perspective but from above, in the sense of being above time, above past, present and future. This leads Boethius to ask:

> Why then, do you think that the things which Providence sees in its eternal present are governed by necessity whereas the things which you see in your present you don't regard as being governed by necessity?

Notice here a problem, which illustrates the point about human attempts to grasp the grammar of a timeless God. The phrase 'eternal present' is a very human phrase. We understand 'present' because we can relate it to concepts of past and future. We might also discuss whether the concept of eternity itself presupposes a way of talking rooted in time. Boethius is struggling with the limits of language, which is why it is helpful for you to take your reading slowly, thinking about each stage in the argument.

Boethius extends this example by saying:

> If we may properly compare God's vision to human vision, He sees all things in an eternal present just as humans see things in a non-eternal present. If you consider divine vision in this light, it follows that divine foreknowledge does not change the nature or the properties of individual things: it simply sees those things as present which we would regard as future.

Boethius asks his reader to think about a man out for a walk on a sunny day. Imagine a viewer sitting on a hill looking down on the walking man. The watcher can conclude that it is both 'necessary' that the sun is shining and that the man is walking, though 'necessary' in different ways. That the sun is shining is part of the way the universe works; at certain times of the day, in certain weather conditions, the sun will always shine. The man has *chosen* to walk, however to the viewer the walking man is *necessarily* walking, because he *is* walking. In the moment he is walking, the man cannot be not walking, because this would be a contradiction. But the act in itself is a free act, as the man chose to walk, yet could have chosen not to do so. The viewer clearly has no influence over the man who is walking or the sun which is shining. To come back to God's knowledge Boethius says:

> The intellect of God is not confused or changeable: He knows all things intuitively, whether these things happen of necessity or not.

It is this comparison of our vision and knowledge with that of God which leads Boethius to say:

> In this manner, the divine mind looks down on all things and, without intervening and changing the nature of the things it is viewing, sees things as eternally present but which, in respect to us, belong to the future.

If God knows '*in advance*' what anyone is going to do then it might still seem that he must take some responsibility for her action. So, for example, knowing in advance that Hitler would kill 18 million people in the Holocaust and not doing anything to stop him would mean that God should, to some extent, be held responsible. If we hold that this is the case, then what right has God to reward or punish anyone?

It is for this reason that Boethius labours this particular view of Divine foreknowledge. If, as he argues, God's knowledge is not ever of the future but is always of the 'simultaneous present', then He cannot be held in anyway responsible for any free human action. Boethius expresses this idea by saying:

> Therefore, when God knows that something is going to happen in the future, he may know a thing which will not happen out of necessity, but voluntarily; God's foreknowledge does not impose necessity on things.

In the same way that the spectator when watching the man walk does not in any way influence the man, God when he sees what all of humanity 'are doing' does not impose his will upon those countless free actions. The watcher has no more influence over the rising and shining sun that he or she does over the man walking. As we have seen, there is clearly a distinction to be made over the way these actions are 'necessary'. To deal with this, Boethius introduces the idea of simple and conditional necessity.

Simple and Conditional Necessity

It is worth restating the examples Boethius himself uses:

> *One is simple, as when we say that all humans are necessarily mortal.*
> *The other is conditional, as when you see a man walking, it is necessary that*
> *he's walking, or else you wouldn't see him walking.*

The key to understanding this view of conditional necessity is for the reader to see that conditional necessity does not imply simple necessity, for it is not caused by the particular nature of an event or choice, but on some condition added to the event or choice. It is easy to see that no necessity forces the walking man to walk; he has voluntarily chosen to move himself forward using his feet. However, as long as the man is walking, he is necessarily moving himself forward using his feet. In the same manner, if God sees anything in His eternal present, it follows that this thing exists necessarily in the way God sees it, but it may not exist the way it does out of some necessity in its nature.

In order to express this in terms of Divine foreknowledge, Boethius says:

> So God sees future things that are the result of human free will; these things, then, are necessary, on the condition that they are known by God, but, considered only in themselves, they are still free in their own natures . . .

So the question is located in the nature of the event or action. When you explore the nature of an action, is it brought about by the way the universe is or does this action contain within it some sort of free choice? As I type this, time is ticking on in its simple inevitable way towards all sorts of deadlines; however the deadlines themselves are brought about by free decisions which I have chosen to make. On the one hand this chapter needs to be finished by a set deadline which may seem to be rushing towards me, but it actually approaches at a fixed rate. The lessons which need to be prepared, the 2010 examination papers which need to be written, the Inset for teachers which has to be prepared, are all now necessities in my life but only through my free choice. In its simple way the sun will shine (or probably not, up here in Scotland) and time will march forward of necessity without any external force moving them. The concept, eventually, is a simple one, though the consequences for our understanding of the nature of God can be profound. God's knowledge of a simultaneous present makes it impossible for him to have any effect on human choices and hence leaves us fully responsible for good or ill actions which we undertake freely.

A good summary of this distinction between simple and conditional necessity can again be found in Boethius' own words:

> The difference between simple and conditional necessity is *the addition of the condition*.

This phrase can be a good way of remembering the position held by Boethius and it is this distinction which allows us to believe both in God's foreknowledge and our freedom at the same time.

To Conclude That God Rewards and Punishes Justly

All this leads Boethius to conclude:

> Since all this is true, we can conclude that the freedom of human will remains completely independent of God's foreknowledge and the laws which prescribe rewards and punishments are just since they provide rewards and punishments for the free actions of the human will rather than reward or punish things that happen of necessity.

Here he returns to his view that as God sees us from above and knows all things in his eternal present; then he rightly judges our future, free actions, and justly distributes rewards and punishments.

Criticisms of Boethius

No one should underestimate the significance of Boethius for the development of thought. He was deeply influential on all medieval thought, as even a cursory study of St Anselm or Aquinas – or Geoffrey Chaucer – will quickly make clear. He worked as commentator on Aristotle, but developed profoundly original ideas, not least as the first philosopher to develop the notion of God as timeless, that is, outside time.

The problems for many philosophers include whether the notion of a timeless God is coherent. According to philosophers of the concretist school, such as Tadeusz Kotarbiński, duration is built into any idea of existence: to be involves some lasting – a duration. To be is to last somewhat. But, as we have argued elsewhere in this book, there is nothing God is like. It is not merely that for God to be loving, knowing and so on, he will be so in a way that surpasses human understanding, but that being itself cannot be understood in any categories we can conceive.

If this is so, then we might ask whether we are justified in making the assumptions about how God perceives which are integral to Boethius' understanding. If the grammar of necessity changes, so too does the grammar of perception. God is not a human viewer on a hillside, with the limits of human perception.

Neither is he a powerless one, at least not as traditionally conceived. When we observe a traffic accident from a distance, we can do nothing about it. But God is seen as omnipotent. Even if we argue, as Aquinas does, that this means that God can do everything logically possible, the limits of that possibility in a spectator God seem so great as to empty – or at least diminish – the concept of omnipotence.

There is also a problem for religious faith. In faith, God is seen as fulfilling a Covenant, a Covenant of being with his people in a pilgrimage – not sitting on a hillside, watching them go by, as a casual spectator watching a military parade. The

God of scripture is a God continually involved with his people. We might ask whether Boethius thinks too much in terms of God being 'up there', on the assumption of a three-tier universe.

For many, such as Process theologians, Boethius, though a Christian, represents the God of Greek Philosophy rather than the living God of Abraham, Isaac and Jacob.

STRETCH AND CHALLENGE

As with many issues and question in philosophy of religion, this is a sophisticated and in some ways convincing answer to a serious question, namely how can we believe in a God who knows of so much suffering throughout his creation and yet does nothing to alleviate or indeed stop this suffering? It is looking for a particular route to solving a problem but, in the process, it may have inadvertently raised other questions which other philosophers thought they had already solved. If philosophers focus too directly on a problem, such as Divine Foreknowledge, they can lose focus on larger questions. A profitable discussion here may, for example, be found in reflecting on the question that if we accept that God is outside time and experiencing everything in a simultaneous moment, than how would Christians explain God becoming incarnate, in Jesus Christ?

Exercise and Examination Advice

Make a list of the following terms in your notes and make sure you research them until you have a clear understanding of what each means:

Time

Eternity

Divine

Foreknowledge

Providence

Prevision

Simple Necessity

Conditional Necessity

Rewards and Punishments

The only actual reading you need to do for this chapter is the short section from **The Consolation of Philosophy** which is on the specification you are studying. However, if you have the time it would be a good exercise to read more of this book to place this chapter in the context of the rest of Boethius' dialogue with Lady Philosophy.

As you will have done with other exercises throughout this course this may be a good time to set up a number of debates which could be rehearsed in groups and then presented to the rest of the class.

You could, for example, split into teams to research different areas of thought and opinion which your team prepares to argue for come what may, e.g.:

- Time as a fixed concept which cannot be viewed from another dimension.
- Necessity cannot be separated from God's will
- We are all determined there is no such thing as conditional necessity
- Time is an illusion
- God is not good.

In these kinds of exercises the less you feel attracted to a particular opinion, the more you should choose it and find ways of arguing for it. Someone who fully understands an issue can argue the ins and outs from any side; those who hold one opinion firmly rarely understand what the debate is really about.

You could then try the following question:

'God has no right to punish people made in his own image.' Discuss.

Body and Soul 11

Introduction

Few subjects have exercised the philosophical imagination more than what it means to be a person. In simple terms, we may ask the question about what it means to be me. Consider our own existence. For the sake of argument, let us assume that there is a real world which contains material objects which we can perceive with our five senses. Among those objects, we see a body which we take to be our own. The hand I see typing these words – I cannot touch-type – I believe to be my hand, the all-too solid body sitting in this chair I take to be my body, and so on; and I believe I see 'me' when I look in the mirror. I give my body a name – I call it 'Michael', and it occupies a space I think of as exclusively mine. I do not share my exact body space with anyone I do not think of as 'me'.

But notice the way our language works. I talk of 'my hand', 'my body' and so on. It is a construction which seems exactly like other phrases I use, when, for example I talk of 'my house', 'my CD collection', 'my cat' or whatever. But is the usage identical? My house is not me – it is something I (and my wife and the mortgage company) own.

My CD collection, tiny though it might be, is something that belongs to *me*. It is something which is not me, but belongs to me. But I speak of 'my hand', 'my body', in the same type of phrase. Is my hand something which *belongs* to me as my CDs do, or is it a part of me? I talk about 'my body' as if it were a possession; if it were a possession, it would not be me, any more than my CD collection *is* me.

Grammar matters here, as it has elsewhere in our discussions. Grammatically, I talk of 'my body', but is that what I really mean? Is there a 'me', which is separate from my body? If there is, what sort of a thing is it? To put it in a very familiar way, is it truer to say that 'I *am* a body', than 'I have a body'? After all, my friends know me as a body – presumably (I hope) as a feeling and thinking body, but a body nonetheless. They recognize me from my face and bulk and the sound of my physical voice. And, if they see me out, they say: 'I saw *you* the other day.' They do not say: 'I saw your body the other day' – at least, not normally.

This would suggest that if there is 'me', it is simply my body. If I think I am really a 'soul' or 'spirit', it looks very much like an error based on the way we speak: 'my body' suggesting that it is something I possess, apart from the real 'me'. If this were the case, then we could simply dismiss any talk of body *and* soul as a linguistic error.

But things are not so simple. There is the problem of actual lived experience. If I were to be dissected, my brain would appear as a gloopy, grey mass, with odd shapes within it. When Lenin died, his brain was razor sliced so that Soviet scientists could – in due course – discover the secrets of the greatest genius in history. What they found was – bits of brain. In those physical bits, not a clue existed about the *mind* of Lenin. And here we find the problem. I do not experience my mind as a gloopy mass. It is, to me, not experienced as a material object. My thoughts and feelings do not come to me as electrical impulses in grey matter. To me they are lively thoughts, feelings, flashes of colour, words, memories, dreams, wishes, hopes, disappointments etc. If a brain surgeon handed me a bit of my brain and told me that was my memories of China, I would not readily see the link between that greyish-pinkish lump and the lived experience of walking on the Great Wall.

Philosophers address these questions in different ways. A key discussion in the Philosophy of Mind is *Mind–Brain Identity Theory*. Are 'mind' and 'brain' simply different terms for the same thing, or is 'mind' somehow different? If so, what is that 'somehow'?

In more traditional terms, the question was the distinction between 'body' and 'soul'. This notion is very significant in religious thought – much religious discourse has been about 'saving souls', the 'eternity of the soul' and so on. The 'soul' is seen, by many, as 'the true me'. It is a fundamental question in Christianity whether God wants to save people's souls. The tendency is to talk of the body as temporary and given inevitably to decay while the soul is eternal. Whether such a view owes more to Plato than to Jesus is much disputed by theologians and philosophers.

Before we look more deeply into these matters, a few terms should be known:

- *Dualism*, which is the belief that we have two elements – body and soul;
- *Substance Dualism*, which holds that these two elements are wholly different substances;
- *Monism*, which is the view that we are one substance, not two;
- *Materialism*, which believes that the only substance is a material one.

There are some more technical bits, but we shall introduce them as we continue our discussion.

The Legacy of Plato and Aristotle

In our AS book (Continuum, 2009), we developed the notion of the soul in Plato and Aristotle at greater length than will be possible here. Nevertheless, it is important to recapitulate key parts of that understanding.

It was common to Greek thought to separate the soul, which was wholly spiritual, from the material body. For Plato, the soul was eternal, not simply because it had no end, but because it had no beginning. It was not capable of destruction, because, as a simple substance it hard no parts into which to disintegrate. For Plato, its true home was in the Realm of the Forms – this body is temporary and corruptible, but the soul would live on.

In important ways, this view was very different from that held by Christianity. The latter denies the immortality of the soul, in Plato's sense. To say that nothing could destroy the soul would be to limit the power of God. The Christian believes that any eternal life which the soul might have is a gift of God. Christianity believes that the soul has a beginning and also that we have one earthly life – the notion of the transmigration of souls, about which Plato speculated, plays no part in orthodox discussions of the soul.

Aristotle disagreed. Like Plato, he was a dualist – there was a distinction between body and soul. But for Aristotle, the soul was the animating principle of the body. The difference between a live body and a corpse is the presence of the soul. When the soul dies, so does the body. The soul is, in Aristotle's sense, the 'form' of the body. But it is not eternal; it dies. Aristotle speculated that perhaps reason, in some form, might continue eternally, but he had no notion of personal survival.

The early Christian Church was deeply influenced by Platonism. It does not mean that Christian thinkers adopted every aspect of Greek thought, but Greek philosophy provided the principal tools for the development of doctrine. The language of scholarship was mainly Greek – the New Testament was written in Greek. People (including Mel Gibson, director of *The Passion*) are often unaware that the language of the Eastern provinces, as spoken by the soldiers, was Greek, not Latin.

The thought pattern, the vocabulary in which religious thought was expressed, was Greek, and the natural point of reference was to think of the human as body and soul: following Plato, it was the soul that was the 'real' me.

From the beginning of the Church, there was the ever-present danger of heresy. The most common type of heresy was to magnify the soul at the expense of the body. Among heresies such as Gnosticism, the body, the material, became something not from God. Only the purely spiritual was of God. In Manichaeanism, there was eternal conflict between the good spiritual god and the evil material one. These views would be echoed over the centuries by groups such as the Bogomils and Cathars (Albigensians). The Church found itself in near – continuous battle with these views. It had to insist that there was one God, creator of all things. The Nicene Creed was created largely in response to these heresies, insisting that God was the Father Almighty (not limited), sole creator of all heaven and earth, things visible and invisible. But even though orthodoxy would triumph (sometimes by quite dreadful methods, as in the Crusade against the Albigensians), the tendency to separate body and soul, to emphasize the corruptibility of the former, even to talk of Christ's mission being to save the souls of mankind, became the common currency of religious discourse. (It is perhaps worth remembering that the Jewish approach did not – and does not – make this radical distinction between body and soul. Neither do the Gospels – Christ's redemption is of people, not souls).

Christianity struggles conceptually with the material. The Reformers railed against what they saw as the gaudiness and materialism of the medieval church, and many struggle with the material side of Christ. In people's imaginations, Christ can become a rarified person, not really human, but faith teaches that he was fully human. That means that he had all the normal bodily functions, and cut his toenails, had sexual desires and needed the privy, like the rest of us. To say such a thing to some seems like blasphemy: but that is what 'the Word was made flesh' means, if it is taken seriously.

St Thomas Aquinas on the Soul

As we would expect, St Thomas Aquinas was very influenced by Aristotle in his view of the soul. Aquinas tells us:

> . . . the soul is defined as the first principle of life in living things: for we call living things 'animate,' [i.e. having a soul], and those things which have no life, 'inanimate.' . . . it is the 'first' principle of life . . . Now, though a body may be a principle of life, or to be a living thing, as the heart is a principle of life in an animal, yet nothing bodily can be the first principle of life. It is clear that to be a principle of life, or to be a living thing, does not belong to a body as a body; because, if that were the case, *every* body would be a living thing, or a principle of life. Of course, a body is able to be a living thing

or even a principle of life, because it is a body. When it is a living body, it owes its life to some principle which is called its 'act'. Therefore the soul, which is the first principle of life, is not a body, but the act of a body; just as heat . . . is not a body, but an act of a body. *S,T*.I, Q.75.a1.c.

Notice that Aquinas is not saying that the soul *is* me. It is the principle of life, rather as Aristotle argued. Life needs the body to be animated. He goes on to argue this more precisely:

. . . the human soul, which is called the 'intellect' or the 'mind', is something incorporeal and subsistent. *S.T*.I, Q.75.a2.c.

It is not material and to be understood as the mind, not something separate from it. The body is needed to be me:

Just as it belongs to the notion of *this* particular man to be composed of *this* soul, of *this* flesh, and of *these* bones; so it belongs to the whole notion of man to be composed of soul, flesh, and bones. . . . Sensation is not the operation of the soul only. As, then, sensation is an operation of man [as a whole] . . . it is clear that man is not a soul only, but something composed of soul and body. Plato, because he thought that sensation was simply a function of the soul, was able to maintain that man was a soul making use of the body. *S.T*.I, Q.75.a4.c.

The sense of the soul being a principle of the whole person, and not something separate, is, as we shall see, interestingly developed in various modern discussions, such as found in Anscombe. Notice, in the last extract above, that Aquinas is very aware of the difference between his view and that derived from Plato.

Substance Dualism: Descartes

Rene Descartes' treatment of the soul, found in both *Meditations* and a less well-known work, *The Passions of the Soul*,[1] developed a view of the soul and its relationship with the body which represented a dualism as radical as that of Plato. The Aristotelian/Thomist view, in which the soul was the principle of life, played no part in Descartes' view. The body and soul were wholly separate substances. In the *Meditations on First Philosophy*, he argues:

There is a very great difference between a mind and a body, because a body is by nature divisible, but the mind is not. Clearly, when I think about the mind, that is, of myself as far as I am a thing that thinks, I am not aware of any parts in me – that is, I understand myself to be one whole person. Although the whole mind seems united to the whole body, if a foot, or an arm, or another limb were amputated from my body, nothing would be taken from my mind. Mental faculties, such as 'willing', 'sensing, 'understanding' cannot be called its 'parts', because it is always the same mind that wills, senses or understands. But any corporeal or physically extended thing I can think of, I can easily think of as divided into parts. . . . This reasoning alone would be enough to teach me that the mind is wholly different from the body. *Meditation* VI.

In *The Passions of the Soul*, Descartes suggests that:

There is a little gland in the brain where the soul exercises its functions more particularly than in the other parts of the body.

In his *Treatise on Man*, he claims that the pineal gland is the seat of the imagination and common sense – here it becomes (perhaps) the link between body and soul. The argument for this function is rather thin: he says that all the parts of our brain are double, and we have also two bodily organs for each sense – two nostrils, eyes, ears [one tongue, but never mind!), but our mind perceives only a single thought or impression. The pineal organ is the bit of the brain that is singular, so it must be the home of the single thought.

The obvious problem here, apart from any uncertainties about physiology, is that simply to pick on the pineal gland leaves open the question of how that physical thing can encompass the non-material thought: the mind–brain identity problem has moved no nearer to a solution.

Gilbert Ryle and 'The Concept of Mind'

A major figure in the British analytical tradition was Gilbert Ryle (1900–76), whose most famous book was *The Concept of Mind*, first published in 1949. In this, he argued that Descartes represented what he called 'the dogma of "the ghost in the machine" ', a vision of the human which made the mind a separate substance somehow attached to the body, acting like the pilot of a ship. The body becomes simply a machine, with the mind the mysterious, non-physical 'real me', like an operator somehow outside that body.

He argues that Descartes is guilty of what he calls a *category error*, by which he meant assuming, incorrectly, that two terms (in this case 'mind' and 'matter') are of the same logical type. They are not, even though sentences about mind and matter might look superficially similar (such as 'there are physical processes' and 'there are mental processes').

He illustrates his point by three famous examples.

1. Suppose a foreign visitor went to Oxford or Cambridge to look at its sights. He is shown the different colleges, the Fitzwilliam Museum, the library and so on.

At the end of the tour, he then asks, 'But where is the University?' He is guilty of a category error – assuming that the University is something separate from and other than all those individual bits which collectively *are* the university.

2. A boy is watching a military parade, in which he knows a Division is marching by. Someone points out to him different squadrons, battalions, batteries and so on. At the end he asks when the Division will arrive, unaware that all the units he has seen are collectively the Division.

3. Consider the foreigner who goes to see a game of cricket, having previously read a book about it. He is shown the stumps and the ball, and the various fielding positions. Then he asks, 'But where is the team spirit?' – a category error. In the same way, Descartes is guilty of a category error because he assumes that sentences about causes, sensations or events must be *either* mental *or* physical, which presupposes an unjustified assumption that they cannot be both.

Ryle's point is, in many ways, not too far removed from the views of Aquinas and Aristotle – for different reasons, they do not make the radical separation of soul and body found in Descartes, Plato and so much of the Western tradition.

We should therefore avoid any mistaken temptation to think of Ryle as some sort of materialist,[2] for he was not. We can be sure of this, because he says so:

> . . . Both Idealism and Materialism are answers to an improper question. The 'reduction' of the material world to mental processes and states, as well as the 'reduction' of mental states and processes to physical states and processes, presupposes the legitimacy of the disjunction 'Either there exist minds or there exist bodies (but not both)'. It would be like saying, 'either she bought a left-hand and right hand glove or she bought a pair of gloves (but not both)'. Gilbert Ryle: *The Concept of Mind*, Penguin 1963, pp. 23–4.

As an analytical philosopher, he is not setting up an alternative metaphysic, but rather seeking conceptual clarity. Indeed, in *The Concept of Mind* he says specifically that he is not arguing that we are simply reducible to physics and chemistry, and in a later work, *Dilemmas,* he gives another of his analogies to demonstrate the irreducibility of things. The accountant audits the books of a university college and claims proudly that the accounts show everything that there is to be said about the college. The bright student who questions him cannot help but think there is rather more to it than can be captured in the figures and formulae, however complete they might appear.

John Hick and Richard Dawkins

If one wants to discover a hard materialist, none comes harder than Richard Dawkins. But it would be wholly mistaken to think of his approach as necessarily as far removed from that of Aristotle and Aquinas as it obviously is from that of Plato and Aquinas. A very straightforward and helpful way of looking at Dawkins' dialogue with Stephen Pinker, sponsored by *The Guardian* and available on the internet (http://www.edge.org/documents/archive/edge53.html – all quotations below are from this source).

Here, as elsewhere, Dawkins distinguishes between two versions of the soul, which he calls Soul One and Soul Two.

He characterizes Soul One thus:

Soul One refers to a particular theory of life. It's the theory that there is something non-material about life, some non-physical vital principle. It's the theory according to which a body has to be animated by some anima. Vitalized by a vital force. Energized by some mysterious energy. Spiritual-ized by some mysterious spirit. Made conscious by some mysterious thing or substance called consciousness. You'll notice that all those definitions of Soul One are circular and non-productive. It's no accident. Julian Huxley once satirically likened vitalism to the theory that a railway engine works by 'force-locomotif.' I don't always agree with Julian Huxley, but here he hit the nail beautifully. In the sense of Soul One, science has either killed the soul or is in the process of doing so.

We can see at once that the definition of the souls as 'vitalized . . . made conscious by some mysterious thing . . . spiritualized by some mysterious spirit' refers very clearly to the type of dualism we have discussed.

Soul Two is very different:

But there is a second sense of soul, Soul Two, which takes off from another one of the Oxford dictionary's definitions:

'Intellectual or spiritual power. High development of the mental faculties. Also, in somewhat weakened sense, deep feeling, sensitivity.'

For Dawkins, Soul Two is real, part of what we are. He admits:

. . . there are, of course many unsolved problems, and scientists are the first to admit this. There are aspects of human subjective consciousness that are deeply mysterious . . . We don't know. We don't understand it.

There's a cheap debating trick which implies that if, say, science can't explain something, this must mean that some other discipline can. If scientists suspect that all aspects of the mind have a scientific explanation but they can't actually say what that explanation is yet, then of course it's open to you to doubt whether the explanation ever will be forthcoming. That's a perfectly reasonable doubt. But it's not legitimately open to you to substitute a word like soul, or spirit, as if that constituted an explanation. It is not an explanation, it's an evasion. It's just a name for that which we don't understand. The scientist may agree to use the word soul for that which we don't understand, but the scientist adds, 'But we're working on it, and one day we hope we shall explain it.' The dishonest trick is to use a word like soul or spirit as if it constituted an explanation.

Consciousness is still mysterious. And scientists, I think, all admit it. . . .

My suspicion, my hunch, my hope, is that . . . [an answer will be found] . . . for the conscious mind. Probably within the next century. Soul One will finally be killed, and good riddance. But in the process, Soul Two, far from being destroyed, will still be finding new worlds to conquer.

. . . Darwinism in . . . [a] . . . general universal sense refers to the differential survival of any kind of self-replicating coded information which has some sort of power or influence over its probability of being replicated. DNA is the main kind of replicating entity that we know on this planet that has that property. When we look at living things on this planet, overwhelmingly the kind of explanation we should be seeking, if we ask what the functional significance is an explanation in terms of the good of the genes. Any adaptation is for the good of the genes which made that adaptation.

Dawkins therefore places his faith in DNA as the source of the answer he seeks. He does not for a moment deny imagination or poetry or any other aspects of conscious life.

Where others would perhaps disagree with him is in his assumption that DNA will be the answer. One must always remain open to the possibility of the unexpected, and because science has answered so many questions about the nature of human life, it does not follow that every answer is even in principle knowable – but neither is the opposite the case.

Where the philosophical believer might take issue with Dawkins is his assumption that religious people necessarily take a narrow, Soul One approach: what we have said already suggests a religious approach which might look beyond a simple dualism. Dawkins accuses religious people of narrow-mindedness about Soul Two:

Well it's common enough for people to agree that religions have got the facts all wrong, but 'Nevertheless,' they go on to say, 'you have to admit that religions do provide something that people need. We crave a deeper meaning to life, a deeper, more imaginative understanding of the mystery of existence.' . . . Religions are not imaginative, not poetic, not soulful. On the contrary, they are parochial, small-minded, niggardly with the human imagination, precisely where science is generous.

John Hick and Other Modern Views

Hick's position is not very far removed from that of Dawkins. He strongly opposes the Platonic view of the soul, not least for assuming that the soul is immortal in itself. For Hick, as for Aquinas, 'my soul is not me'. His outlook is not dissimilar to that of Aristotle, and is often described as 'soft materialism'. We are our bodies, but those bodies have a spiritual dimension. This is why, as we shall see, when he considers the notion of afterlife, he adopts his replica theory: that is, when we die, God creates a replica of ourselves in a resurrection world.

Hick especially opposes an approach which assumes that to die is something without fear. For Plato's Socrates, as the soul cannot die, death is nothing particular to fear. To go from death to life is simply like moving from one room to another. But for the Christian, to die is to be before God – he alone can bestow eternal life.

Hick's view (though not his Replica Theory) is supported by many other believers. G. E. M. Anscombe,[3] following Wittgenstein, considered the phenomenon of pointing. If I point at something, the mere action of the body is not the whole of its meaning. If I point at the king on a chessboard, my bodily action is what it is – a gesture. But the meaning of the gesture, that I am pointing out that it is this piece here, and not that bishop, or that I am indicating that it is this colour, or has this texture or design feature, cannot be indicated by that bodily gesture alone. But neither are we able to claim that the pointing is by an immaterial substance – it is my body that points. She argues that 'this bodily act is an act of man *qua* spirit', the act of a human as a whole.

In a similar way, Herbert McCabe sees the soul in terms of the significance and *meaning* of the living being. It is not something separate from it. If life consists in the being alive, then, following Aristotle, that is what we mean by the soul.[4]

Perhaps we can leave a final word to another believer, Peter Geach:

It is a savage superstition to suppose that a man consists of two pieces, body and soul, which come apart at death; the superstition is not mended but rather aggravated by conceptual confusion, if the soul-piece is supposed to be immaterial. The genius of Plato and Descartes has given this superstition an undeservedly long lease of life; it gained some accidental support from Scriptural language, e.g. about flesh and spirit – accidental, because a Platonic-Cartesian reading of such passages is mistaken, as Scripture scholars now generally agree. In truth, a man *is* a sort of body, not a body *plus* an immaterial somewhat; for a man is an animal, and an animal with one kind of living body; and thinking is a vital activity of a man, not of any part of him, material or immaterial. The only tenable conception of the soul is the Aristotelian conception of the soul as the form, or actual organisation, of the living body. . . . Peter Geach: 'What Do We Think With', *God and the Soul*, 2nd Edition, St Augustine's Press, p. 38.

Exercises and Examination Advice

Make a list of the following terms in your notes and make sure you research them until you have a clear understanding of what each means;

Mind–Brain Identity Theory

Dualism

Substance Dualism

Monism

Materialism

Plato's understanding of soul

Aristotle's understanding of Form (in this context)

Aquinas' understanding of soul

Incorporeal

Subsistent

Dualism in Descartes

The pineal gland

The ghost in the machine

What Gilbert Ryle meant by Category error

You should also be able to demonstrate a good understanding of the views of writers such as:

Plato

Aristotle

Thomas Aquinas

Rene Descartes

Gilbert Ryle

Richard Dawkins

John Hick

This chapter has introduced you to a number of concepts which are not always easy to understand in a single reading but they are essential not only for a good understanding of this part of the specification but because some of the ideas in the next chapter will build on the work you have done here. It is worth spending the time to make sure you understand all the subtleties of the issues involved.

A useful discussion, for example, to develop the Aristotelian concept might be to explore the difference between a car with and without its engine running. To make the engine run you do not need to add anything to the car – these days it is often just a process of pressing a button. The car will be much more useful with the engine running but it has gained no material to make it happen. Then debate whether or not the difference between a living and dead body is the same with evolution or

God pressing the button. (Keeping in mind, as with many of the science and religion debates in the AS course, is it legitimate to compare organic and non-organic 'machines'?).

You could also work on the dualist debate, in the Cartesian sense – if we have a soul which is a ghost in a machine, how does it interact with the machine? For those with the time and interest, and a liking for stretch and challenge, you could also read up on the work that Roger Penrose is doing to explore whether or not there is any evidence that consciousness takes place at the quantum level.

For those who, like me, enjoy the philosophical problems aired through Science Fiction, the Terminator series of films and television shows are based on the fear that making computers more and more complex and 'intelligent' will eventually make them 'self aware' and the consequences are seen as dire for the human race. There are many debates to be had here; from the question of what we mean by intelligence, to what exactly does it mean to be self aware, to the very human question behind much of this debate 'Are we more than the sum of our parts?'

While I would never be allowed to set a question as interesting as *'Are we more than the sum of our parts?'* it would be a good one to try to answer as a conclusion to the study of this section. I say this because any good response will include a consideration of all that you will have learned from your work on this chapter.

Notes

1. Descartes, Rene (1596–1650) (1998) 'The Passions of the Soul', In: *Selected Philosophical Writings*, Translated by: J. Cottingham, R. Stoothoff and D. Murdoch (Cambridge University Press: Cambridge, England), pp. 218–38.
2. An error sometimes perpetrated by writers too idle to read what he actually says.
3. G. E. M. Anscombe (2006) 'Analytical Philosophy and the Spirituality of Man', *Human Life, Action and Ethics*, Imprint Academic, pp. 3–16.
4. See, e.g. Herbert McCabe (2008) *On Aquinas*, Continuum, *passim*.

Life after Death 12

Any belief system which talks about life after death will be based on having come to a conclusion about the 'mind–body' or 'body–soul' debate. An understanding of these issues therefore is essential for the following debates in philosophy. In this part of the specification you will be expected to know the meaning of several concepts: resurrection, reincarnation and disembodied existence. You will need to be really careful to make sure you do know what philosophers are saying and not assume that you know. I think of this as the Three Kings assumption. Many young people starting gospel studies will insist that the infancy narratives talk about three kings; in fact I have seen some putting more effort into finding them than they are willing to put into their homework. There is, of course, no mention of the three kings in the New Testament.

Resurrection

Assumptions about resurrection can be misleading. Many Christians, for example, think of a body dying and a soul being resurrected in some heavenly place. However, in the Apostles Creed, an early summary of Christian teachings, you will read:

> I believe in the Holy Spirit, the holy *catholic church,
>   the communion of saints,
>   the forgiveness of sins,
>   *the resurrection of the body,*
>   and life everlasting.'
> (*Note: In this context, catholic means 'universal' not 'Roman Catholic')

This early teaching is quite clear that Christians should believe in bodily resurrection and that they believed that life everlasting would be a bodily experience.

Centuries later the definition of resurrection as the rising again from the dead, the resumption of life, was firmly stated for Christians by the Fourth Lateran Council which taught the following:

> . . . all men, whether elect or reprobate, 'will rise again with their own bodies which they now bear about with them'. In the language of the creeds and professions of faith this return to life is called resurrection of the body for a double reason: first, since the soul cannot die, it cannot be said to return to life; second the heretical contention of Hymeneus and Philitus that the Scriptures denote by resurrection not the return to life of the body, but the rising of the soul from the death of sin to the life of grace, must be excluded.[1]

It is natural to ask what exactly a risen body would be like and whether there is really any philosophical justification for the belief. Before looking at modern views, the Fourth Lateran Council again gives us some good ideas.

They believed that everyone would rise from the dead in their own, in their entire and in immortal bodies. However, those who had lived good lives could expect to rise to a resurrection of a life in heaven, whereas those who had lived evil lives would face a resurrection of Judgement. The Council fathers believed that it would destroy the very idea of resurrection if the dead were to rise in bodies not their own. Later, we will look at Replica Theory by John Hick which is a *thought experiment* designed to see whether bodily resurrection is possible.

The risen bodies of both saints and sinners, however, will be different in that they will be immortal bodies. The justification for this view that Christ has triumphed over death is taken from a number of places in scripture, e.g.:

. . . he has destroyed death forever. (Isaiah 25: 8)

. . . and the last of these enemies he has done away with is death. . . . (1 Corinthians 15:26)

Good as this is for the saved, the other side of the coin will not be of so much fun for those who are to be punished; as to be punished in this sense you must have a body. In Revelation 9:6 we read:

> When this happens, people will long for death and not find it anywhere, they will want to die and death will evade them.

Some may argue that these teachings come more from a desire to control than to expound theology, but it is clearly a dogma which needs bodily resurrection to make it meaningful.

The theology surrounding these three characteristics, identity, entirety and immortality, was seen to be common to the risen bodies of the good and the wicked. The difference was that the bodies of the saints would be distinguished by four transcendent endowments, often called qualities.

The first of these is known as 'impassibility'. This meant that the risen bodies of the just were placed beyond the reach of pain and inconvenience. In Pauline terms, what was 'sown' in corruption will on rising be incorruptible (1 Corinthians 15:42). On the other hand, the bodies of the others will also be incorruptible but not 'impassible' meaning that they will be subject to a great deal of pain.

The next quality, again building on the writings of St Paul is to do with 'glory' or 'brightness', by which the bodies of the saints shall shine like the sun. Paul writes:

> The sun has its own splendour, the moon another splendour, and the stars yet another splendour, and the stars yet another splendour; and the stars differ among themselves in splendour. It is the same too with the resurrection of the dead. All the bodies of the saints then will be equally impossible, but they will be endowed with different degrees of glory.

In heaven the saved will all be glorified, but in different ways which will require a body to be expressed.

The third quality making use of the Pauline view which says: '. . . what is sown is weak, but what is raised will be powerful.' (1 Corinthians 15:43) is taken to mean that the saved will have a greater agility, in which the body will be freed from its slowness of motion, and given the ability to move with the utmost facility and quickness wherever the soul pleases.

The fourth quality is almost akin to the reverse of Platonic thinking on body and soul. In this world, the soul is held back by the carnal appetites of the body. Now, the body becomes subject to the absolute dominion of the soul. According to Paul:

> . . . what is sown is a natural body, and what is raised is a spiritual body' (1 *Corinthians* 15:44).

The body will now participate in the soul's more perfect and spiritual life to such an extent that it becomes itself like a spirit itself. The example to justify this view is that after his resurrection, Christ passed through material objects, such as walls, even though he clearly had a body – emphasized by its still having holes from the nails on the cross and the spear in his side, and his being touched by Thomas.

The Beatific Vision

Thomas Aquinas wrote only a few decades after this council, and was faced with the challenge of trying to reconcile this view of bodily resurrection with that of the Aristotelian philosophy which would permeate his and other Western philosophical writings. To do this, he had to use what Peter Vardy and Julie Arliss call a modified dualism. The soul for Aristotle was not a different thing but what makes that thing what it is. Aquinas wanted to hold this view of the soul while also saying that the soul separated from the body at the point of death. Vardy and Arliss neatly summarize this problem in two points:

1. If whatever survived was my soul, then my soul would be me and this is a dualist position which Aquinas rejected.
2. If the soul were not me, then I would not survive death.

Peter Vardy and Julie Arliss: *The Thinkers Guide to God*.

To resolve this, Aquinas seems to hold that there is a time when the body and soul are not united but that the soul is somewhere lacking its fullness, and waiting to be reunited with a glorified body. This leads to Thomas to postulate a Beatific Vision as the ultimate goal of human existence. This can be reached only after physical death and the soul being reunited with this glorified body. Aquinas' formulation of beholding God in Heaven may parallel Plato's description of beholding the Good in the world of the Forms. It does however return the idea of the soul being the form of the body to an existence in a heavenly realm. Aristotle and early mediaeval theology appeared united.

Replica Theory

As we saw in the last chapter, John Hick was convinced that it made no sense to speak of the person without a body. The first challenge was therefore, if he was to maintain a belief in the afterlife, how a resurrection of the dead might be possible. Secondly, he was asking specifically what St Paul meant by the resurrection of the dead. We have one account above, from the Fourth Lateran Council, and Hick gives us another when he says:

> His conception (Paul's) of the general resurrection . . . has nothing to do with the resuscitation of corpses in a cemetery. It concerns God's re-creation or reconstitution of the human psychophysical individual, not as the organism that has died but as a **soma pneumatikon**, 'a spiritual body', inhabiting a spiritual world as the physical body inhabits our present physical world. John Hick: *Philosophy of Religion*, Second Edition, Prentice Hall, 1973, p. **100**.

The implicit problem in this model, which is not addressed by St Paul, is one of personal identity. If I want me to be in another world or dimension or heaven, how is this going to happen, what counts as me, and how will I be recognized by my family and friends? It was to address this issue that John Hick developed the replica theory which he neatly splits into three parts, building from a simple account of what might be me to a possibly resurrected me. In the first part he proposes:

> Suppose, first, that someone – John Smith – living in the USA were suddenly and inexplicably to disappear from before the eyes of his friends, and appear in India. The person who appears in India is exactly similar in both mental and physical characteristics to the person who disappeared in America. There is continuity of memory, complete similarity of bodily features including finger prints, hair and eye colouration, and stomach contents, and also beliefs, habits, emotions and mental dispositions. Further, the 'John Smith' replica thinks of himself as being the John Smith who disappeared in the USA. After all possible test have been made and have proved positive, the factors leading his friends to accept 'John Smith' as John Smith would surely prevail and would cause them to overlook even his mysterious transference from one continent to another, rather than treat 'John Smith' with all John Smith's memories and other characteristics, as someone other than John Smith. John Hick: *Philosophy of Religion*, Second Edition, Prentice Hall, 1973, p. **100**.

In this first part of the example, Hick has set up a clear idea of what people might look for if they were trying to decide what would count as personal identity in this kind of case. How do you prove you are still you to people who know you really well? Some friends might focus on different criteria in the list and many would want to know what memories you had of them which would be personal to the two of you. In a similar way to the first premise of Anselm's Ontological argument, once you have accepted the possibility of this move, then the next follows quite easily. This time Hick suggests:

> Suppose, second, that our John Smith, instead of inexplicably disappearing, dies, but at the moment of his death a 'John Smith' replica, again complete with memories and all other characteristics, appears in India. Even with the corpse on our hands we would, I think still have to accept this 'John Smith' as the John Smith who died. We would have to say that he had been miraculously re-created in another place. Ibid. p. **101**.

Here Hick make a natural move from asking his readers to accept a kind of 'beam me up Scotty' case to a situation where the man has actually died before reappearing elsewhere, and this time he has left a corpse behind. This is clearly closer to the experience of death with which we are all familiar. Notice, however, that he has no empirical evidence for the reappearance outside the thought experiment and makes no allowance for the way a person might have died. He leaves himself open to the question of what kind of body we might have if we had, for example, been run over by a bus.

Finally Hick moves onto:

> Now suppose, third, that on John Smith's death the 'John Smith' replica appears, not in India, but as a resurrection replica in a different world altogether, a resurrection world inhabited only by resurrected persons. This world occupies its own space distinct from that with which we are now familiar. That is to say, an object in the resurrection world is not situated at any distance or in any direction from the objects in our present world, although each object in either world is spatially related to every other object in the same world. Ibid. p. **101**.

We now have the complete picture of Replica Theory, an attempt to explain how it might be possible to believe in '*God's re-creation or reconstitution of the human psycho-physical individual*'. It is not hard to see the flaws in this thought experiment and much has been written about what age the replica might be, whether it would be physically challenged if the original was and it would be damaged if the person's death had been violent. Added to these are the ideas put forward by Peter Vardy and others of the value of 'copies'; if God can make one copy, why not make hundreds? I find a mirrored reflection difficult enough without the thought of hundreds of 'mes' walking around. Finally, among these common critiques of the experiment, many have pointed out that a copy of the Mona Lisa is not the same as the real thing and therefore not as valuable in any sense of the word.

Much has been written about this theory over the years and John Smith has disappeared and reappeared in a remarkable number of places. It is important to be clear firstly that this is a thought experiment and one which Hick himself does not believe necessarily works. But it has created a valuable debate which has broadened the way we can think and talk about God and personal immortality.

Disembodied Existence

The possibility of disembodied survival after death cannot be considered without taking into account the nature of the human person. A common way of considering these issues would seem to be that mind–body dualism is a 'survival–friendly' view supporting life after death, whereas materialist views make this kind of survival impossible. One of the main critiques of belief in this view of life after death is that we have no legitimate idea of what would count as criteria for being able to identify one another if we were disembodied. Another aspect to the problem is that we have no idea what existence with no body might be like: we have no experience of being ourselves without a body. Some may talk about 'out of body' experiences but they are still talking of 'seeing' the environment around them, including other people (friends, family or doctors) and 'hearing' their voices or even music in the operating theatre.

This challenge of what this kind of existence might be like was taken up by H. H. Price in an article in 1953. Price explores in some detail what disembodied existence might be like. He proposes a world where disembodied 'souls' exist as some kind of dream images. These images, we are asked to imagine, are shared between a number of more or less like-minded, and telepathically communicating, souls. These images would have to include some kind of image of their own body and consequently other people's bodies. It would be hard therefore, in the beginning, to see the difference between our world and the 'image world'.

This is an attractive approach as we all know what it is like to dream and we also know that moving from one place to another in a dream is easy and often instantaneous. It can be imagined and does give us a legitimate language with which to consider disembodied existence.

As I mentioned above, one of the discussions often heard, namely that of out of body experiences, adds to the possibility of this being at least a conceivable approach. A number of other books cover the story of Pam Reynolds who had to have a brain operation which meant turning off all the brain activities for the duration of the procedure. There is no point in telling the whole story here, but the interesting question is where does consciousness take place? If she really did experience seeing doctors and hearing music and voices without brain activity, how is this possible? Are we really dealing with a soul which can function as a personality without a body? One interesting possible alternative, which is being explored by scientists like Sir Roger Penrose, is whether or not consciousness takes place at a quantum level still functioning below, and therefore not needing brain activity. This takes us back into earlier questions of dualism, such as whether there is a relationship between a soul and a body and how do they interact?

Reincarnation

It is worth looking at Hindu teachings. Before doing this though, we should note that Hinduism is not a single religion but a grouping together of a great variety of religious ideas which grew together into what may be best described as a family of religions.

In fact, some cynics have described Hinduism as a British construct created to describe religious people in the Indian subcontinent who are neither Muslim nor Christian. This however falls short of seeing the rich and varied religious beliefs which make up this colourful religion. It is a religion which can move from the heights of spiritual mysticism, a belief system which can contemplate a union between the soul and a personal God who created and controlled the universe, to a religion which at the same time holds the most basic myths and superstitions. Hindus can be monotheistic or polytheistic, pantheist or even in some cases atheist. This makes it very difficult to tie down Hindu beliefs. That said, some beliefs are held in common, and it is from these that we find the information to understand reincarnation.

Hindus would hold that their earliest scriptures, the *Vedas*, come directly from God. They believe in continuous creation, which means the conservation and dissolution of the universe in a cyclic form. This leads to a belief in what they call the 'transmigration of souls' according to the law of eternal consequences known as *karma-samsara*. This leads to a hope of the final liberation of the soul from the chains of transmigration, known as *moksha*.

It is this idea of the transmigration of the soul which leads to the concept of reincarnation, sometimes known as rebirth or *palingenesis* – to begin again. This concept can be summarized as believing that the soul or eternal Self moves through a series of bodies which most often may be human or animal, though they may be divine. This belief is not limited to the Indian subcontinent, but it can be found all over the world and may be as old as humanity itself. To understand this way of thinking, we need to see human beings as composed of two fundamental principles opposed to each other in their nature; the soul or *atman* and the material body or *sharira*. For Hindus, the *atman* is not born or created but is eternal and immutable and therefore indestructible. The body, however, is, as we all know from the empirical evidence, temporal, mutable, destructible and, for Hindus, created.

There is then no need for the *atman* to have a body and the joining can be seen as accidental. The joining is a kind of imprisonment brought about by *avidya* and *karma*, with which the *atman* is associated from all eternity. *Avidya* means ignorance, or individual ignorance. According to *Sankara*, *avidya* is endless, but it can be ended at any moment when a human attains spiritual enlightenment. *Avidya* is believed to cause man to move further away from the Self and obscure his knowledge of the truth. The *Bhagavad-Gita* says that all sufferings and limitations imposed by the ego come from *avidya*; therefore man needs to seek knowledge, with which hatred and greed are incompatible.

This leads to the concept of *karma* which, for Hindus, explains causality through a system where good effects can be derived from past good actions and bad effects can be brought about by actions in one's past. This creates a system in which actions and reactions continue through a person's reincarnated lives. It is important to understand that *karmic* actions and consequences create 'habits' or patterns of thinking, which determine the realm in which the Self is reincarnated, rather than it being a totting up of each individual *karmic* consequence.

Reincarnation, then, is a dualist system with all the philosophical questions attached to dualism. A major critic of such an outlook is Peter Geach. In his essay, 'Reincarnation'[2], he argued that even the experience of continued memories between different bodies would not be sufficient to claim the same identity, for such 'memories' could be accounted for in other ways, and memories can be mistaken. (People can even attribute to themselves memories that are actually those of others. George IV in old age gave lengthy accounts of his observations at the Battle of Waterloo, though he was in Brighton at the time, and Ronald Reagan is said to have believed himself, seriously but erroneously, to have been at the D-Day landings). But in reincarnation, neither the continuity of body nor of memory is necessarily claimed, and it is difficult therefore to make sense of the idea that it represents continued existence.

The Problem of Evil and Life after Death

This clearly brings together a number of threads which have been running through your course. This means that any question for this section of the specification could be approached using knowledge and understanding of theodicies, of dualism, of monism or even the philosophy and ethics of Kant.

Monism, naturally, does not have much to say on the topic. If a writer is a materialist, like Richard Dawkins, there is no life after death and no route to a resolution of the problems raised for the God of classical theism, by the suffering and evil throughout this world. Of course, if you were answering a question from this part of the specification you would need to be clear why writers such as Dawkins believe what they do and there is more than enough information earlier in the book for a full response to any examination question.

While heaven and hell are no longer on the OCR specification, a consideration of their meaning is useful in understanding the issues surrounding finding a solution to the problem of evil in a belief in the afterlife.

As you know from the theodicies you have studied, an afterlife is assumed, even taken for granted, by the philosophers who seek to justify a loving God who allows evil to exist. Irenaeus, for example, is arguing that we are not born perfect but called to be perfect. There would be no point in this theodicy if there were no afterlife. If there were no God calling us to become 'in his image' and giving us the time to do this, then all the suffering that many people have to undergo would be meaningless; and Christians would indeed have a God who is not worthy of worship.

Another approach to this topic would be to use the work of Kant, particularly the *summum bonum*. Again, there is no need to cover the same ground in detail. What you will need to do is take the knowledge and understanding you have gained earlier in the course and see how it adds enlightenment to this topic. If morality is truly rational and all men deserve justice then we must be immortal, in an after*life* sense and we need the aid of a benevolent deity.

STRETCH AND CHALLENGE

Predestination

One of the areas of philosophy which is full of nuanced difficulty is predestination. An interesting exploration from which you could gain a great deal from would be to look at the implications for life after death and indeed for the concepts of life after death of predestination. You could read some of the works of John Calvin, or other reformers, and explore whether or not anyone who believes in predestination can find comfort in thought of an afterlife if she might have been predestined for an eternity of punishment.

Questions about predestination are closely tied to questions of God's knowledge. If the future as it exists to us is eternally present in God's mind then in what sense can that knowing be considered the same as determination? How does this relate to questions about the mercy of God? Is it a merciful to create someone in the full knowledge that perdition is to be that soul's fate? We return to the way in which the questions we have considered interrelate: to ask questions of this kind shows the problems of dealing with – from our limited perspective – the qualities and the unknowable mind of God.

D. Z. Phillips and Immortality

Dewi Phillips provided an alternative – and to many believers, too reductionist – view of the meaning of eternal life. In a significant little book, *Death and Immortality*,[3] Phillips developed the idea that eternal life is not a temporal concept. By this, he was attacking the idea that 'eternity' – in the religious sense – means 'endless time' Wittgenstein had argued that 'Death is not an event in life – we do not live to experience death'.[4] By this he meant that death cannot be experienced – experience presupposes the continuation of life after the event, so that the event becomes an experience, consciously held. Phillips further analyses the notion of human actions and relationships, claiming that the nature of relationships – which are an important part of us – is predicated upon mortality.

For him, eternal life means a quality of this life, a being with God, not a man's continued survival after death. He argues:

> The immortality of his soul has to do, not with its existence after death and all the consequences that is supposed to carry with it, but with his participation in God's life, in his contemplation of divine love. D. Z. Phillips: *Death and Immortality*, Macmillan, p. 38.

For Phillips, what matters is the type of person one is: eternal life consists in being, now and in this world, a person filled with the love of God:

> The immortality of the soul refers to the state an individual is in in relation to the unchanging reality of God. It is in this way that the notions of immortality of the soul and of eternal life go together. Ibid., p. 55.

Whether such a view makes sense of the nature of belief and the knowledge of, and knowledge of the nature of God, at least for the vast majority of believers, is perhaps too complex to consider all at once. Perhaps it is for another day – and another book.

Exercises and Examination Advice

Make a list of the following terms in your notes and make sure you research them until you have a clear understanding of what each means;

Resurrection

The resurrection of the body

Life everlasting

Replica Theory

Thought experiment

Impassibility

The Beatific Vision

Soma pneumatikon

Psychophysical individual

Disembodied existence

Reincarnation

Fourth Lateran Council

You should also be able to demonstrate a good understanding of the views of writers such as:

John Hick

Thomas Aquinas

Vardy and Arliss

H. H. Price.

By this final chapter, you will be well aware of all the different exercises you might try both to broaden you understanding and prepare for the examination on this topic. Here you could, perhaps, research the different ideas about disembodied existence. You could, for example, research, in groups, different types of evidence for out of body experiences. Having looked at the evidence ask yourselves, does it in fact amount to the proof that we are more than our bodies or is there a scientific explanation which is more likely based on chemical reactions in our brains? In other words, does the evidence point to a reductionist view of humanity or a view that can only be interpreted as a body and spirit combined?

Finally ask yourself:

To what extent do we need bodies for our personalities to survive into the next life?

Notes

1. *The Catholic Encyclopaedia* (2008), Vol. 12 (New York: Robert Appleton Company), November <http://www.newadvent.org/cathen/12792a.htm>.
2. Peter Geach (1969) 'Reincarnation' in: *God and the Soul* (St Augustine's Press), pp. 1–16.
3. Macmillan, 1970.
4. *Tractatus Logico-Philosophicus*, 6.4311.3.

Appendices

Appendices

A. Writing Philosophy Essays

Introduction

Philosophy is examined principally through the essay, and Philosophy examiners reward candidates who construct sound essays. These notes are designed to help you towards good writing.

It is important to notice that Philosophy examining is *not* primarily about testing knowledge, but about judging how well you can deploy interpretation, analysis and explanation to produce a coherent argument. The essay is a particularly good means to see your abilities in these fields: if knowledge alone were the goal, multiple choice or short answers would be a better test.

Starting the Essay

The essay is always an attempt to answer a question. Sometimes the question is explicit: e.g. 'Does Descartes establish a convincing case for mind/body dualism?' Quite often the question is implied: e.g. '"Descartes' attempt to create a convincing dualism of mind and body was a failure" Discuss.' In the latter case, the question is whether you agree or disagree with the quotation. The most important point to notice is that the question, whether open or concealed, is *not* 'Write down everything you know about Descartes and the mind-body problem'. And a question requires an answer. If someone asks you where to get a bus to the town centre, he is not asking you to give him the history of the town centre, or a discussion of the state of public transport. The only relevant answer is one that tells him where to get the bus.

It is tempting to avoid answering a question from the beginning: many essays on the subjects above will begin:

> Descartes was a famous French philosopher and mathematician who wrote *Discourse on Method* and *Meditations*. In *Meditations*, he used the method of doubt. Wondering whether it was possible to be certain about anything, he began with 'I think, therefore I am'. This was an important step in sceptical philosophy, and began the modern interest in questions of epistemology.

So far, the examiner has no thought but a doubt about whether the candidate has read the question. The content is not objectionable in itself, but has made no mention of *any* material demanded. The candidate has failed to establish relevance to *this* question.

A much better answer might begin like this:

> In *Meditations*, Descartes presents a dualism of mind and body, believing that they are quite different things. A key problem of dualism is how the very different body and mind are connected with each other and how they interact. It is difficult to see how a purely mental, non-physical event, such as a thought, can cause an action in a material body.
>
> Descartes' dualism follows from his belief that . . .

In this example, the candidate has immediately tried to deal with the question. The terms of the question are dealt with in the first sentence, and the problems that need to be addressed are clear from the first two sentences – mind and body are different things, and there is a question of how they interrelate. Notice how the third sentence opens up the question by showing exactly what the problem is, and how it uses the brief example of a thought as a mental event. Importantly, the writer has *defined* the nature of the problem. Careful definition is crucial: the examiner wants to know precisely your understanding of technical terms such as 'dualism'. The second paragraph will tell us why this problem is acute in Descartes, and successive paragraphs will, we may assume, deal with how well he copes with the difficulties. These paragraphs must remain on the subject, and build towards an answer.

The Body of the Essay

Each point you make must add towards an answer; do not 'pad' with material not required by the question.

A problem for some students is that they make a list of points, and then write a paragraph on each, like a shopping list. It is important, when you have a list of points, not just to *give* them, but to indicate their relevance and links. Paragraphs need to refer to each other: this can be done in a phrase or two, perhaps at the start of the paragraph. Useful phrases to do this can be: 'A further supporting argument is . . .'; 'Perhaps the most powerful argument against this is . . .'; 'Many reasons may be given in support of this view, but perhaps crucial is the idea that . . .'. There needs to be something at the start of each paragraph to indicate that the previous one exists as part of your argument.

The key is that you are arguing towards a conclusion, and not simply listing points. The examiner wants to see that you have *weighed* different points of view, *assessed* the more from the less significant, and really are working to a conclusion, which means that as you work towards the end, you are telling him how you weigh points as you go along.

It is important to notice that examiners are concerned with whether you are *considering* opinions, not merely listing them. They want to know what you think about them, and why. Many weaker candidates think that their list becomes an argument by using 'however, *x* says . . .' before each listed theory, with no evidence of consideration of the arguments advanced.

In this part of the essay, remember to give examples to explain your argument in practice, and to show your understanding. This will be rewarded by examiners.

The Conclusion

Schoolteachers tend, when teaching how to write essays, to say 'Always write a conclusion'. This advice is correct, but it can be misleading.

It is tempting to write all the points one wishes to make, and then to add on a conclusion. This is an error, to be avoided. It is true that the final paragraph should leave the reader in no doubt as to the answer you wish to give to the question, but this is best done by leaving your strongest argument to final paragraph, as the clincher:

What counts most against Descartes' view is . . . For this reason, his account is ultimately unconvincing, as he cannot deal adequately with the problem of . . .

Points are being added, with no doubt as to your view. Be bold enough to have a view, where it is requested.

There are two horrors to avoid. One is the conclusion which begins 'In conclusion' and goes on to list some banalities which are unconnected with the points you have made. It is obvious that this is your conclusion – this is the final paragraph – and this type of ending looks like an afterthought of someone who has run out of ideas. Keeping a strong, clinching point for the final paragraph demonstrates that you are still thinking. The worst form of conclusion is the one which says:

> x is a very difficult problem which has baffled philosophers for thousands of years, and will doubtless be discussed for centuries to come.

This tells the examiner that the candidate has decided not to venture an opinion, because thinking is hard. The examiner set the question to receive a considered opinion, not to be told, at the end, that you have given up thinking for the day. If you cannot give a firm answer to a question – and this is perfectly respectable philosophically – you must do the reader the courtesy of saying why – in your considered opinion (not a vague feeling) – this should be so.

Ask yourself, at the end of whatever you write, 'Have I answered this question?' It doesn't matter whether the examiner agrees with your answer: what matters is that it *is* an answer, to which every paragraph and every sentence has contributed.

The Language of Essays

Be careful with how you write the material. Avoid jokes, just in case the examiner does not share your sense of humour. Avoid slang, not merely the obvious sort ('Kant was wicked', when you mean he was rather a competent thinker), but the less obvious. 'Feel' when you mean 'think' is an obvious one here. Many candidates write 'feel' or 'felt' for 'think' or 'thought'. A moment's reflection shows why this is an error. What I *think* about going to the dentist (it is necessary for dental and general health, and hence a good thing) may be very different from what I *feel* about it (indifference, or, for some, sheer terror). Thought and feeling are very different modes of cognition, and it is sloppy to confuse the two.

Avoid trying to sound too clever by using needlessly long words (you might get them wrong) or writing endless sentences. Seek a natural style. Do not, as some candidates have done, invent words to sound clever. A few years ago, one candidate used 'protagonised' throughout his paper, instead of 'said', 'thought' or 'wrote' ('Kant protagonised that . . .'). It looked silly, not impressive. A clue to a natural style is to *listen* to what you write. If you would wish not to hear something, it is likely you are not expressing it well. Listening to your sentences helps also with punctuation.

B. Revision Notes

The notes here are not intended to be used as a substitute for your own course notes: they are a supplement, drawing attention to key points for revision.

From the Specification

Religious Language

Candidates should be able to demonstrate knowledge and understanding of:

- religious language – uses and purposes;
- the *via negativa* (Apophatic Way);
- the verification and falsification principles;
- different views on the meaningfulness of religious language;
- the uses of symbol, analogy and myth to express human understanding of God; and
- the views of the Vienna Circle, A. J. Ayer, Anthony Flew, Ludwig Wittgenstein and Paul Tillich on Religious Language.

Religious Language

- The key issue is how finite language can encompass an infinite God
- If we say God loves me, then it cannot be expressed in the way that a human does. Can it therefore have any meaning to say this?
- The key distinction is that between **cognitive** and **non-cognitive** language
- **Cognitive sentences** are those about which it is appropriate to ask whether they are true or false – 'Berlin is the capital of France' is false but cognitive
- **Non-cognitive sentences** are those about which it is inappropriate to ask whether they are true or false – curses, commands, poetry etc. would come under this category
- It is a matter of great argument whether religious sentences are cognitive or not

Via Negativa (The Apophatic Way)

- Often associated with John Scotus Eriugena (c.810–c.877) and Moses Maimonides (1135–1204)
- Argues that we can say nothing positive about God, because we cannot begin to comprehend him
- All we can do is to say what God is not

- This preserves the dignity of God – very important in Maimonides' Jewish tradition
- BUT to say what something is not is surely to say something positive about God. To say he is not a penguin, or is not ignorant, implies something positive. Negative sentences have degrees of positive entailment

Analogy

- Most often associated with St Thomas Aquinas (1224/5–1274)
- Aquinas accepted the significance of the apophatic way in preserving the unknowable essence of God, but argued that we could be more positive than that
- Distinguishes *analogical* from univocal (word used in two sentences with identical meaning) and equivocal (word used in two sentences with entirely different meanings) usage
- Two types of analogy – *attribution* where from the health of the bull's urine we impute health to the bull, though the health of each is quite unlike the other, and proportion: we love proportionate to our nature, God proportionate to his
- A useful illustration is Baron von Hügel's example of the loyalty of a dog. It is nothing like loyalty in a human, but we see enough in common to use the term of the dog. That is a 'downwards' analogy: we look upwards to God
- Aquinas is clear that the Doctrine of Analogy tells us *how* we are using language, not what it *means*
- Ian Ramsey argues in *Religious Language* (1957) for 'qualified models'. This is based on disclosure situations (as more sides are added to a polygon it eventually is experienced as a circle). In a qualified model, the key word acts as a model for the reality it represents, while the qualifier shows that the key word is only a model. If we describe God as *First Cause*, 'cause' is the model, but 'first' shows that God is not a cause like other causes. Ramsey essentially is being more precise about analogy
- The key problem of analogy, pointed out by Geach and others, is how we can judge the legitimacy of the analogy when one of the comparators is unknown. How can we say God is like *x* when we have no knowledge of God to judge the aptness of the comparison?

Symbol

- Paul Tillich (1886–1965) is main proponent
- Distinguishes between a sign and a symbol
- A sign (such as a pointing finger) is simply a convention pointing to something outside itself
- A symbol points towards and participates in that to which it points
- An example is a national flag, such as the Stars and Stripes, which stands for the USA but is also part of that nation
- Symbols have lives of their own – the 'Stars and Bars' continues to resonate over a century after the state it represented disappeared
- Religious symbols are affirmed and negated by that to which it points. 'God is Love' is true, because he is, but is false also because God's love is far more than anything we can mean by the words
- BUT does symbol clarify language any more than analogy? Is all language about God so obviously symbolic – do the more technical theological terms resonate with us as 'God is Love' does?
- J. H. Randall Jr. takes a non-cognitive view of symbol
- Arguing that symbols, like art, open up aspects of ourselves which cannot be reached in any other way
- They open up 'the order of the divine' which does not necessarily coincide with the existence of an objective order
- BUT Christians generally treat their language cognitively

Myth

- It represents a very complex understanding of symbolic language
- Modern approaches do not treat myths as untrue but as means to deep insights to human experience
- They play an important part in the life of communities which have a view of the religious interpretation of existence
- Perhaps the most important scholar is Rudolf Bultmann (1884–1976) who argued for the demythologising of scripture to find the *kerygma* which is to be understood in existential terms. Jesus lived fully in the face of his death and showed us how to do the same

Another Non-Cognitive Analysis

- R. B. Braithwaite (1900–90) argues that religious language is fundamentally a statement of ethical intent
- 'God is Love' ≡ 'I intend to act in an agapeistic way'
- What distinguishes religions is the psychological support given to these ethical demands by the associated stories
- It is irrelevant whether these stories are true: Bunyan's *Pilgrim's Progress* has profoundly changed British religious life
- BUT many religious sentences are not obviously ethical commands or stories
- Also it demonstrates poor logic. If I hold that God is Truth, but I intend to lie in given circumstances, a position that does seem conceivable, it would be translated in Braithwaite's usage as 'I intend not to tell a lie but I intend to lie' which would be absurd, so the proposed translation does not hold

Incarnational Meaning

- John Hick argues that Christianity has a potent clue to understanding religious language
- God was incarnated in Jesus
- This enables us to see fairly precisely what God's qualities mean in human terms
- Jesus' love becomes a sign of God's love

Verification and Falsification

- The challenge of verification was first made by the Vienna Circle (Logical Positivists, led by Moritz Schlick (1882–1936), Rudolf Carnap (1891–1970) and Otto Neurath (1882–1945))
- Main English proponent A. J. Ayer (1910–1989) in *Language, Truth and Logic* (1936)
- The only significant propositions are those which are either tautologies, so true by definition (these include the truths of mathematics, which are tautological as reducible to $x = x$), or which are empirically verifiable. All other sentences are meaningless
- A distinction is made between conclusive verification (*strong verification*) which is unachievable as no sense experience can be conclusive, and *weak verification* which argues that one must be able to state what experiences would make a statement probable. Ayer adopts the latter
- Religious statements are held to be unverifiable and therefore meaningless. According to Ayer, 'there is a God', 'there is no God', 'Is there a God?' would all be meaningless
- Logical Positivism was challenged by Karl Popper (1902–94) in *Logik der Forschung* (1934)
- Argues that verification principle is meaningless by its own rules

- Notes that we do not learn by continually trying to find sentences true, but by attempting to falsify them and producing better hypotheses
- The mark of genuine science is that it is highly falsifiable
- But not being falsifiable does not make a sentence meaningless – it is just not science
- Anthony Flew (1923–) in the *University* debate issued the challenge to believers that they forever qualify their view so that God 'dies the death of a thousand qualifications' and asks whether anything could count against their beliefs. He cites John Wisdom's analogy of the gardener
- R. M. Hare (1919–2002) argues in favour of *bliks*, unfalsifiable and unverifiable beliefs (hence non-cognitive) which nevertheless profoundly change the nature of people's lives
- Gives the example of the student who believes all the dons are out to kill him
- We all have bliks. The only difference between ourselves and the student is that his blik is insane
- BUT Flew argues that Christians treat their statements as genuinely cognitive
- Hick has subsequently objected that it makes no sense to call a blik sane or insane: the claim for a blik is that nothing can count for or against it, so a judgement about sanity makes no sense
- Basil Mitchell (1917–) argues that religious sentences are cognitive, even though we may not be in a position to verify them
- Gives the example of the partisan who meets a stranger who claims to be leader of the resistance
- Urges the partisan to believe in him even though evidence will be ambiguous – at times he seems like a collaborator
- Argues that we accept that there is evidence against belief, but that we have reason for it – a belief about the character of the stranger
- Hick has subsequently glossed his parable by arguing that a) the stranger presumably does know whether he is telling the truth; b) when the war is over, the truth will emerge (he is looking forward to his own notion of eschatological verification)
- Richard Swinburne has argued (*The Coherence of Theism*, 1977) that some sentences are unverifiable and unfalsifiable but have meaning. Gives the example of toys in the cupboard that come alive when there is no-one about
- John Hick uses the parable of the Celestial City
- Argues for Eschatological Verification
- Christianity has specific afterlife beliefs. If we find when we die that what we find matches what we expected, we would then be in a position to say we were right all along
- After all we need to be in the right place to verify experiences
- But of course these things are verifiable in principle if true, but not falsifiable if false
- But this does meet the challenge of weak verification

Language Games

- Associated with the later thought of Ludwig Wittgenstein (1889–1951) in *Philosophical Investigations* (1953) and the *Blue and Brown Books* (1958)
- Language Game theory argues that the only use of language is within language games
- Words do not have absolute meanings, only the meanings they have within the game
- To know the meaning of a word is to know its use within the game
- There are only the games: to try to get outside them would be simply to play another game
- The games do not reflect reality – they make it
- Each game is a form of life
- So, religious language takes place within the game: we can only clarify its meaning
- Wittgenstein's disciple J. L. Austin (1911–60) developed the idea of *illocutionary* use, arguing that it is important to examine what language *does* as well as what it *means*
- Wittgenstein has profoundly influenced many within Philosophy of Religion, including Don Cupitt, Rush Rhees, Peter Winch and D. Z. Phillips

- Peter Geach has argued that Language Game theory is essentially circular. The word takes its meaning from the game, but the game gets it meaning from the words within it. There needs to be something external on which it rests

From the Specification

Experience and Religion

Candidates should be able to demonstrate knowledge and understanding, in relation to God and religious belief, of:

- arguments from religious experience from William James;
- the aims and main conclusions drawn by William James in *The Varieties of Religious Experience*;
- the following different forms of religious experience: visions, voices, numinous experience, conversion experience and corporate religious experience; and
- the concept of revelation through sacred writings.

Experience and Religion

Religious Experience

- Religious experiences may be of many different kinds
- For many, like St Paul, conversion experiences are key to their lives
- Some argue that prayer provides a subtle but real religious experience
- Some experience voices – they claim to hear God speaking to them
- Others, such as Julian of Norwich, Hildegard of Bingen, Teresa of Avila, Meister Eckhart, claim to be shown visions of God
- St Teresa argues that a sign of authenticity is that the visions are in accordance with the belief of the church and that they are genuinely life-changing
- Rudolph Otto (1869–1937) in *The Idea of the Holy* (1917) stressed God as 'the wholly other'
- Devised the term 'numinous' (from the Latin *numen* – 'divinity') to refer to the nature of the experience
- Described Religious experience as *mysterium tremendum et fascinans*
- Martin Buber (1878–1965) in *I and Thou* (1937) stresses personal relationship with God (I–Thou), which moves beyond I–It relationship: a personal encounter
- Modern Interest in Corporate Experiences such as the Toronto Blessing
- Classic account comes from William James (1842–1910) in *The Varieties of Religious Experience*
- Identifies four common strands to religious experience:
  ○ Noetic quality – goes beyond any normal experience revealing something quite other
  ○ Ineffabilty – cannot be expressed in available words
  ○ Transiency – normal time stands still
  ○ Passivity – we are taken over
- All this is taken by some as evidence of God especially because there is a common core to these beliefs
- BUT sincerity of those experiences does not guarantee veracity
- People can be honestly mistaken, drunk, hysterical etc.
- The privacy of experience is a problem – how do I know your experience?
- Freud would blame need for father figure/ritual/Oedipus Complex/fear of unknown for experience

- Would argue that Teresa of Avila's 'visions were obviously sexual in origin
- Marx would look at wish-fulfilment, opiate of people etc.
- Are these experiences like sense experience? God is not material, not a person like other people
- How could we recognise a non-physical, infinite God with our finite minds?
- Some argue these experiences are self-authenticating, but the key issue here would be privacy of experience
- Some argue that there is no God so religious experience are *ex hypothesi* impossible
- That not everyone experiences them counts against them
- Corporate experiences could be explained by a kind of mass hysteria and perhaps the manipulation of mood by charismatic preachers
- An issue is that they do not always seem biblically authentic. The gift of tongues in *Acts* is that everyone can understand what the apostles say, not that they gabble incomprehensibly
- Richard Swinburne (1934–) in *The Existence of God* (1979) argues for The Principle of Credulity (If someone says *x* is present to them, *x* probably is present unless we think there are good reasons to think otherwise) and The Principle of Testimony (people should be believed unless there are good reasons not to do so.)
- Hobbes argued that if I say God spoke to me in a dream I might as easily argue that I dreamed that God spoke to me

Revelation and Scripture

Propositional Views

- These are based on the view that the content of revelation is God revealing certain truths
- Faith becomes acceptance of those truths
- The truths may be found in particular formulations. In Islam the key is the Holy Koran, for fundamentalism it is the literal word of scripture
- For others it might be certain truths in scripture, the Creeds and the *magisterium* of the Church (Roman Catholicism), or, e.g. in Lutheranism, in scripture, the Creeds and The Confessions of the Reformers such as Melanchthon (note that these views do not necessarily entail a literal reading of scripture)
- This view tends to make a division between Natural and Revealed Theology
- Fundamentalists and evangelicals tend to refer to Scripture as the Word of God, though there is the problem that the Bible is not self-authenticating. Critics argue that this type of religion has the danger of bibliolatry
- This point of view is often described as 'belief that . . .'

Non-Propositional Views

- Emphasize the notion that what is entailed is personal belief in God: what matters is personal relationship
- Referred to as 'belief-in'
- Revelation becomes God revealing himself in history
- Faith becomes our reaction to that self revelation
- This approach tends to reject the Natural/Revealed dichotomy in theology
- The key to scripture is not that it is 'the words of God' – it is rather the witness to the event of God, written from the perspective of authentic acceptance of that message
- John Hick argues that in Scripture the term 'Word' applies to Christ himself (see *John*, 1) – 'In the beginning was the Word and the Word was with God and the Word was God')

- Hick also argues that the method of constructing the Bible at Nicea (325) was in line with the non-propositional view. What was essential to acceptance of the New Testament was that the books had to come from the circle of Jesus and were written from the perspective of faithful acceptance of his nature
- An advantage of this view is that it permits a wide range of interpretations of scripture
- A problem with this view is that surely any belief about God entails some beliefs about him. Faith in someone does surely include certain factual beliefs. To answer Bonhoeffer's question, that the key question to God is 'Who are you?' not 'What is He?', surely entails propositional elements – *that* he is God, *that* he is all-loving etc.

From the Specification

Miracle – a study of how God might interact with humanity, by looking at the concept of miracle.

Candidates should be able to demonstrate knowledge and understanding of:

- different definitions of miracle, including an understanding of Hume;
- the biblical understanding of miracle and the issues this raises about God's activity in the world';
- the concept of miracle and the criticisms made by Hume and Wiles; and
- the implications of the concept of miracle for the problem of evil.

Miracles

- There is a problem of definition. Some argue simply for an event religiously interpreted
- Many take David Hume's view that miracles involve an intervention in the natural laws by the agency of a supernatural being
- Hume argues that miracles are by their nature highly improbable
- Natural Laws are inductive generalisations based on countless instances and *ex hypothesi* are highly probable
- A miracle – a breach of those laws – is therefore by definition highly improbable
- A wise man proportions his belief to the evidence, believing the probable and disbelieving the improbable
- Hume offers 4 subsidiary points;
  - Miracles are rarely witnessed by educated men of good repute
  - They tend to be found in barbarous and ignorant nations
  - The miraculous is more likely to be explained by error, drunkenness, honest mistake etc.
  - Miracles are found in all religious traditions: appear to cancel each other out
- Against Hume, we can argue that high probability does not count in favour of a theory – see Popper
- Hume's inductivism is questionable. According to Popper we formulate theories by the *hypothetico-deductive method*. Genuine science is highly falsifiable – we should not seek to prove but to disprove
- Hick takes up this point, arguing that exceptions indicate the need to reformulate the original hypothesis
- In any case, to say *x* is highly improbable does not entail that it is impossible
- Hume's other arguments can be dealt with relatively easily
- Maurice Wiles (1923–2005) in *God's Action in the World* (1986) argues against Hume, pointing to the problems of his account

- Argues that the problem with miracles is essentially theological rather than philosophical, running against the problem of evil (see above for explanation)
- A God who turns wine to water or performs other trivial and apparently arbitrary acts but does nothing about Auschwitz or Hiroshima would not be worthy of worship and would be acting against his own nature
- There is one original miracle, that of the creative act, but no others
- Notes that Jesus refused to prove his own powers by working miracles on demand
- Against those who point to the Resurrection as a miracle essential for Christianity, Wiles argues in *Reason to Believe* (1999) that the resurrection is to be understood symbolically, in terms of the raising of people to new life – cites Hans Küng in support of this view

From the Specification

Attributes

Nature of God

Candidates should be able to demonstrate knowledge and understanding of:

- God as eternal, omniscient, omnipotent and omnibenevolent – and the philosophical problems arising from these concepts;
- The views of Boethius in his discussion of eternity and God's foreknowledge in Book 5 of *The Consolation of Philosophy*; and
- The question as to whether a good God should reward and punish.

Attributes – The Nature of God

Eternity

- The extent to which God can be describes as Timeless
- The extent to which God's existence is everlasting

God's Foreknowledge

- Does God know in advance of our actions?
- Or is he a timeless God who knows everything simultaneously?
- '. . . the perfect possession of boundless life which becomes clearer by comparison with temporal things'

Necessity

- There are two kinds of necessity, one which is simple, for example the sun will rise tomorrow and one day we will all die
- The other is conditional, conditional necessity does come from the nature of an event but is added to it
- The difference between the 2 necessities is the 'addition of the condition'.

God's Justice

- Since God cannot affect our freely chosen behaviour, he too is free to reward and punish us for our decisions

From the Specification

Life and Death – The Soul

Candidates should be able to demonstrate knowledge and understanding of:

- distinctions between body and soul, as expressed in the thinking of Plato, Aristotle, John Hick and Richard Dawkins;
- other concepts of the body/soul distinction;
- different views of life after death; resurrection and reincarnation;
- questions surrounding the nature of disembodied existence; and
- the relationship between the afterlife and the problem of evil.

Life and Death – The Soul

Body and Soul

Plato (427–347 BC)
The Soul:

- a simple substance, has no parts and is therefore indestructible
- has existed for all eternity and will exist for all eternity
- different from Christian conception where such a conception would limit the power of God
- body is temporary and will decay
- true home is realm of the Forms, which we forget because of trauma of birth
- this is a classical *dualist* theory

Aristotle (384–22 BC)
Body and Soul:

- Also a dualist
- Distinction between Form and Substance:
  - Substance is what the chair is made from; it is in the form of a chair
  - Form is immanent, not transcendent – each chair is/has its own form
- Soul is the form/animating principle of the body
- When the body dies, so probably does the soul
- Intellect might survive but not ourselves as persons

St Thomas Aquinas (1224/5–74)

- argues that 'I am not my soul'
- influenced by Aristotle and the Christian belief in resurrection of the body
- full personhood requires body and soul

Descartes (1596–1650)

- takes a sharply dualist view
- the essence is clearly the mind, whose existence can be treated as certain to ourselves
- treats the body as something controlled by the mind
- link might be the pineal gland
- body is machine-like with muscles as pulleys

Gilbert Ryle (1900–76)

- Not a materialist. He says we are not reducible to physics or chemistry. All he is doing is to attack dualism of the Cartesian type rather than offering an alternative of his own
- Accuses Descartes in *The Concept of Mind(sic)* (1949) of treating the soul as 'the ghost in the machine'
- Argues that dualists are guilty of a *category error* treating the soul or mind as a separate object
- Gives the example of the foreigner who goes to Oxford, is shown all the colleges etc. but asks 'Where is the University?' or who goes to a cricket match and asks 'Where is the team spirit?'
- All mind states can be translated into sentences about behaviours

John Hick (1922–)

- adopts a soft materialism
- mind and body are different but mutually dependent
- to be a person involves both

Richard Dawkins (1941–)

- takes a hard materialist view
- we are bodies only, genetically driven
- 'bytes and bytes of digital information'

Life and Death

- There are various theories of afterlife
- Hard materialists tend to reject any thought of afterlife
- For *Dawkins*, the only afterlife is the continuation of our genetic material in our children
- Dualists often accept some form of afterlife
- *Plato* believes that the eventual life is in the Realm of the Forms
- Plato suggests the possibility of reincarnation with the transmigration of souls until freed from this world
- Some religions adopt a belief in *Reincarnation*
- Problem with this is the specific nature of reincarnation
- What do we need to be the same person?
- This is normally thought to involve at least one of *Continuity of body* or *Continuity of Memory* or *Continuity of Personality*
- The question is complicated as none of these is fixed even within one life
- But in Eastern Religions, none seems to give continuity – the identity characteristics all seem absent in Hinduism, and even the soul does not continue in Buddhism

- Geach argues that the memory is not enough
- Christianity believes in *Resurrection* as a single act
- The Creeds specify *Resurrection of the Body* as well as of the soul
- There is a problem. If Aquinas is right, we need our bodies to be fully persons in the afterlife.
- But where would they be? In what state would we be resurrected? As old, sick people or in a throwback to some peak time?
- St Paul assumes some form of resurrection body, glorified in some perfect way (would this still be me?)
- How is there continuity with a rotting corpse or ash left behind on earth?
- John Hick suggests his Replica Theory: God could at the moment of our deaths create a replica in a resurrection world
- Bernard Williams and others argue that this would still be a replica, just as a perfect copy of the *Mona Lisa* would still be a copy
- Non-physical resurrection faces all the problems of dualism (above)
- If Ryle and Dawkins are right there is nothing separable to be resurrected
- Some Christian philosophers take other views
- H. H. Price takes the view of eternity as involving disembodied minds communicating by telepathy
- Rudolf Bultmann argues that afterlife beliefs are mythological
- D. Z. Phillips argues that eternal life is not a temporal concept – it refers to a quality of this life. Our only eternity is for our will to be remembered by God

The Problem of Evil

- The classic problem outlined by Epicurus is the inconsistent triad:
  - God is all-powerful and there could abolish evil;
  - God is all-loving and would wish to abolish evil
  - But evil exists
  - Therefore God is not all-powerful or not all-loving or both
- Two problems: moral evil, the harm humans knowingly do to others: non-moral evil (suffering, natural evil) from earthquakes, floods disease etc.
- Attempts to deal with evil and God called 'theodicies'
- Christianity rejects attempts to argue evil is not real
- St Augustine of Hippo (354–430) – soul-deciding theodicy
- Argues that God created everything good in its own way
- Evil is the going wrong of something itself made good (*privatio boni*)
- Evil caused by creatures rejecting God, first at Fall of Angels then at Fall of Adam and Eve
- Free will has real consequences in human suffering
- The fabric of the world went wrong because of these choices
- Hence natural evil
- We deserve to suffer because we were all seminally present in the loins of Adam
- Evil is either the consequence of sin or punishment for sin
- BUT raises the question of whether a perfectly good creation could go wrong
- Being omnipotent and all-knowing, God could foresee the evil and prevent it
- Presupposes very literal reading of scripture
- Loins of Adam scientifically questionable – assumes homunculi
- God seems punitive
- St Irenaeus (c.130–c.200) – soul-making theodicy, further developed by John Hick (1922–)
- Believes this is a good world for soul-making involving challenges etc.
- Accepts free-will defence
- Real actions must have real consequences
- Earth is especially good for developing character, giving opportunities for virtues like courage, charity, patience etc.

- Hick adds *epistemic distance* – God must leave us a space to be ourselves and to be genuinely free to choose him
- If God kept intervening to stop evil there would be no space for us to develop science and be genuinely free in relation to God
- God wants our love to be freely given
- Hick believes suffering can be justified by the joy of eternal love, which all may achieve – hell would be a place of temporary cleansing like Catholic notion of Purgatory.
- BUT if all go to heaven why give free will in first place
- God could give genuine choice of eternal life or extinction
- Does a loving father simply allow children invariably to suffer evil for the good it might do?
- Richard Swinburne suggests God puts evil into the fabric of the world to teach us the breadth of our capabilities
- God wants us to be great – true greatness involves ability to great harm as well as great good
- God does not make a toy world for little people
- To those who suffer at the hands of others, Swinburne says they have one consolation – they are *of use* to others as moral opportunities: the worst human fate would be to be useless
- To these theodicies the central question has to be whether it speaks to the one who suffers – does the mother in the gas-chamber with her baby feel of use? How does God answer her?
- Hans Küng says God can only answer us by suffering as we do by the Crucifixion
- Process Theology uses idea of panentheism in which all things are contained in God who is 'The Great Companion, the fellow-sufferer who understands' (Alfred North Whitehead)
- D. Z. Phillips attacks instrumental treatments of God – the man who falls among thieves between Jerusalem and Jericho is not there as a moral opportunity for the Good Samaritan. A loving father does not leave children playing on the railway-line as an opportunity for moral development. The consolation God gives us is as Love – the covenant that he is with us. 'Eternal Life' is not a temporal concept

Heaven and Hell

- The key issue is whether views of heaven and hell are compatible with the God of classical theism
- There is an underlying assumption that an afterlife is possible
- The key issue is probably the problem of evil (see below)
- Hell is a particular problem
- In Augustinian theodicy there is a question of whether God created hell, at odds with the notion of the going wrong of an all-good creation
- In Irenaean theodicy as treated by Hick, an eternal hell would serve no soul-making purpose
- In Aquinas, hell is a separation from God – it is not seen in fiery furnace terms
- Modern Catholic theology tends to use the idea of hell as a voluntary rejection of God
- Some theologians have adopted an annihilationist thesis for hell
- Heaven creates some problems
- Traditional versions lack clarity: Aquinas argues that the heavenly state is perfect contemplation of God, perhaps a too Aristotelian view
- Christianity faces the problem of a traditional belief that there is no salvation outside the Church
- At the Second Vatican Council, Roman Catholicism argued that all men of good will are in greater or lesser communion with the Church. This seems consistent with Karl Rahner's notion of 'anonymous Christians' and Pope Benedict XVI's removal of the concept of Limbo
- To many Christians, Catholic notions of Purgatory are unbiblical, but Hick has adopted a similar view (see above)

C. Suggestions for Further Reading

This book builds on our AS book, but is still an introductory text to the subject. It is not, and is not intended to be, a compendium of all that can be said or all that needs to be said on an endlessly fascinating subject. Good students will always read beyond their textbook, looking for new angles and opinions. What we hope to provide here is a guide to further sources, and the occasional health warning.

Internet Sources

On matters philosophical, the Stanford Encyclopedia of Philosophy (*http://plato.stanford.edu*) is most reliable unlike certain entries in the popular *Wikipedia*. On religious matters, *www.newadvent.org* is very useful, not least because it contains a huge collection of translated texts, including the entire *Summa Theologicae*, and many classic texts of the Fathers of the Church. It also has the elderly but interesting, *Catholic Encyclopedia.*

Other valuable resources

www.philofreligion.homestead.com/index.html
http://www.earlham.edu/~peters/philinks.htm#philosophers

These provide useful further links.

Background to Philosophy

It is important to have access to a sound encyclopedia of philosophy to ensure accuracy on key points. *The Oxford Companion to Philosophy*, the *Cambridge Dictionary of Philosophy* and the *Routledge Concise Encyclopedia of Philosophy* and *Routledge Shorter Encyclopedia of Philosophy* may all be confidently recommended.

Especially valuable as an inexpensive reference book is: Anthony C. Thistleton: *A Concise Encyclopedia of the Philosophy of Religion*, Oneworld.

For the History of Philosophy, F. C. Copleston's nine-volume History remains a superb resource. Bertrand Russell's *History of Western Philosophy* needs a health warning. It is excellent on the British Empiricists, but misleading and frequently downright wrong on those with whom he had little sympathy – including Aristotle and Aquinas. On Aquinas, Copleston's Penguin introduction remains excellent, and Brian Davies' *Aquinas* (Continuum) is a valuable modern source. A useful outline is *The History of Christian Thought* by Jonathan Hill (Lion). At a deeper level, there is much to savour in: *The Oxford Handbook of the Philosophy of Religion*, edited by William J. Wainwright (OUP). A wide range of issues is discussed by distinguished contributors, including Peter von Inwagen, Philip Quinn and D. Z. Phillips.

Good anthologies are invaluable. Brian Davies has provided *Philosophy of Religion: A Guide and Anthology* (Oxford) and more contemporary readings may be found in Taliaferro and Griffiths: *Philosophy of Religion: An Anthology* (Blackwell). Steven M. Kahn and David Schatz: *Questions About God* (Oxford) contains a valuable collection of extended extracts from contemporary philosophers. There is also much useful material in John G. Cottingham's excellent *Western Philosophy: An Anthology* (Blackwell). This contains substantial extracts, including – among others – Ryle on the 'ghost in the machine', each fully and carefully introduced.

Introductions to the Philosophy of Religion

There are several good and a number of suspect sources. A very sound text is Brian Davies: *An Introduction to the Philosophy of Religion* (Oxford). Still valuable, but over-priced, is John Hick: *Philosophy of Religion* (Prentice Hall). In more depth, Anthony O'Hear's *Experience, Explanation and Faith* (Gregg – pricey) raises a range of important questions in a readable style. Wide-ranging, thoughtful and often very amusing, is T. J. Mawson's *Belief in God* (Oxford).

An interesting alternative view, much more nuanced and rigorous than anything by Dawkins on religion, is Robin Le Poidevin's *Arguing for Atheism: An Introduction to the Philosophy of Religion* (Routledge).

No-one has done more than Peter Vardy to take the study of philosophy of religion into schools and colleges. There is much that is valuable in both *The Puzzle of God* (Fount) and *The Thinker's Guide to God* (with Julie Arliss – O Books), but they are marred by misleading material about realism and antirealism. Peter Cole has also produced some helpful introductory material (Hodder).

Surprisingly popular are the books by Sarah Tyler and Gordon Reid. Although frequently very well-presented, they contain major errors of philosophical under-standing, and should be avoided, especially for the areas covered in the present text. The understanding of religious language is flawed beyond rescue.

Reading Further

The range of possible further reading is enormous. Some stimulating writers include Richard Swinburne (start with *Is There a God?* (Oxford)), Anthony Kenny (try *The Unknown God* (Continuum)), D. Z. Phillips (more difficult than some, but try Chapter 3 of *The Problem of Evil and the Problem of God* (SCM)), and Herbert McCabe (wonderfully elegant – try *God Matters, God Still Matters*, or *On Aquinas* (all Continuum)). Despite the complexity of ideas, there is marvellously lucid philosophy to be found in Peter Geach: *God and the Soul*, from St Augustine's Press.

A very interesting – and very readable – alternative approach to the Philosophy of Religion is offered by John Cottingham in his fascinating *The Spiritual Dimension: Religion, Philosophy and Human Value* (Cambridge University Press). His *Why Believe?* (Continuum) contributes significantly to many of the debates in this book.

A very approachable book, with a much wider range of topics than its title might imply, especially in its 2008 second edition, is Vincent Brümmer's *What Are We Doing When We Pray?* (Ashgate).

If you are particularly interested in questions of non-realism, look at Eberhard Herrman: *Religion, Reality and a Good Life* (Mohr Siebeck) or Karin Johannesson: *God Pro Nobis: On Non-Metaphysical Realism and the Philosophy of Religion* (Peeters). Neither is easy, but the former is marginally the more straightforward.

If you are interested in some of the points raised by D. Z. Phillips, his *Religion and the Hermeneutics of Contemplation* (Cambridge) is worth dipping into as it deals with such a wide range of issues. It repays slow and thoughtful reading, once you have read other books in the subject.

An interesting, unusual and thoughtful approach to a wide range of topics by one of our younger philosophers of religion can be found in various writings by Mark Wynn. A good place to begin is his: *Emotional Experience and Religious Understanding* (Oxford).

Such background is provided by John Macquarrie: *God-Talk* (SCM) which, unfortunately, appears currently out of print. An available introduction to this area – and generally very recommendable – is Jeff Astley: *Exploring God-Talk: Using Language in Religion* (Darton, Longman and Todd).

Journals

There are several journals designed for those beginning the study of philosophy. There are often useful pieces in *Think*, published by the Royal Institute of Philosophy, as well as in *Philosophy Now*, and *The Philosopher's Magazine*.

Dialogue often contains very useful introductory material on the Philosophy of Religion. The Phillip Allen publication, *Religious Studies*, though very glossy, cannot be recommended for Philosophy of Religion topics, as it frequently contains significant errors, though it is stronger elsewhere.

At a higher level, the principal forum is: *Religious Studies: An International Journal for the Philosophy of Religion* (Cambridge), or, online, the free *Ars Disputandi: The Online Journal for Philosophy of Religion* (http://www.arsdisputandi.org/). Both contain useful material. An interesting innovation is *Oxford Studies in Philosophy of Religion*. Intended as an annual publication, the first volume in 2008 contained material on, among others, miracles, the problem of evil and an excellent article by Peter von Inwagen on Divine Foreknowledge – all pieces directly relevant to the subject of our book.

Read, explore, enjoy, reflect, and keep alive this most fascinating debate.

Index